ENDORSEMENTS

Finally, we have a book not only explaining the watchman but giving watchmen direction. God ordained us each to have a garden where we can watch and worship. For some, your garden is your home. For others, it might be your city, your state, or even your nation. His Ekklesia Kingdom leaders must stand in the gates and displace the authorities of hell that have somehow found their way to rule in positions of influence. In **Wielding the Axe**, Dr. Thomas Schlueter has created a wonderful manual to help us understand how our prayers become strategies for war. Ecclesiastes 10:10 speaks about the impact of a dull axe. As you read this book, get ready not only to sharpen your axe but to wield it in triumph ahead!

Dr. Chuck D. Pierce, Apostle
President, Glory of Zion International Ministries
President, Global Spheres, Inc.

This is an extraordinary book. To read it stirs one up to be a warrior and victor. You will not be able to remain passive nor complacent after you read it. Its words release a fire shut up in your bones. As Christians, we all need to read **Wielding the Axe**; maybe at intervals in our walk with the Lord to keep the fire burning.

Dr. Cindy Jacobs, Apostle
Generals International
Reformation Prayer Network

If the annual Texas State Fair, held in the Fair Park section of Dallas, ever needs someone to fill in for "Big Tex", I nominate Dr. Thomas Schlueter. He is a man of huge stature both in the natural and spiritual realms. His life and ministry are making a major impact on Texas and our nation at this critical time in history.

Tom models servant-leadership in the Kingdom of God. He is a team player, and he knows how to connect and mobilize the Body of Christ for strategic prayer assignments. His catalytic anointing facilitates the flow of the Holy Spirit and enables the accomplishment of the mission. Tom understands that the Ekklesia Church must first be family before it can be an army to deal with the powers of darkness. We can be family and not be an army; but we cannot be an army without being 'a band of brothers.'

The Ekklesia Church is the earthly representative legislative government of the eternal Kingdom of God. It is maturing in history so that the purposes of the Lord God can prevail in history. The keys of the Kingdom will prevail over the gates of hell in a time-space world as

the Ekklesia steps into its governing assignments!
Wielding the Axe defines these assignments and rallies the people of God to enter into the fray! The battle for the earth we are now experiencing is being fought at three major levels. They are: (1) Globalism versus Nationhood; (2) the Cultural War; and (3) the Political War. Use this well-written 'war manual' for personal edification and education, and as an equipping tool to train fellow-soldiers.

Jim Hodges, Apostle
Founder and President of the Federation of Ministers and Churches International
Duncanville, Texas

The wisdom, humility and authority with which Tom Schlueter prays and teaches is why so many trust his leadership. As you read **Wielding the Axe** you will see time and again Tom's faithfulness to carry out the assignments given to him and the Texas Apostolic Prayer Network (Movement). This dedication is one reason he is able to speak with such authority to the Ekklesia today with this Heavenly directive. As someone who has seen the effects and direct impact of the TXAPN prayer he leads in Austin, I can tell you that not only is this a "now" word, but it is also a "now" strategy. Thank you, Tom for listening and being obedient to the Holy Spirits voice.

Trayce Bradford
TXAPN Governmental Specialist
Vice President of Christians Engaged (christiansengaged.org)
Former President of Texas Eagle Forum

As a member of the Elders at the Gates group here in Arlington Texas, I have had the privilege of experiencing first-hand every Tuesday morning, the level of apostolic authority and prophetic insight and discernment that my dear friend Thomas Schlueter has received from the Lord. I have seen the effective use of the axe as a weapon of war against the enemy in our prayer's assignments and intercessions under his leadership. What you read in this book is not theory, is a practical manual that will equip and empower you to fulfill your call to take the fight to the enemies of His Kingdom and storm the gates of Hell. Wield the Axe!

Jorge E Lorenzana
Antioquia International Ministries, Arlington, Texas

As the Church, the Ekklesia, we have entered into a now strategic time of a New Era that many have been prophesying. The message within the pages of this book is a clarion call to prophetic warriors, intercessors, leaders and believers who have a passion for and who are destined to be history makers. Ones who seek His face, carry His glory and who will walk united with others in a grassroots movement of divine strategies to usher in awakening and transformation in cities, regions, states and our nation. Tom, has effectively done just this, birthed and launched an apostolic movement in the state of Texas that is stewarding and ushering in a move of God. As he so eloquently states, "It is imperative in this hour that all of us evaluate the assignments that the Lord has given us, and how he intends to use all of us, individually and corporately, to carry out his Kingdom mandates in order that we might see a transformation and an awakening in our nation that has never been seen before." Learn and glean from this general and apostle how to birth, launch and build a formidable kingdom army, covenanted to the Lord and one another, that will awaken the prophetic destiny of a nation and release heaven on earth. Thank you, Tom, for this now word.

Rebecca Greenwood, Apostle
Christian Harvest International, Cofounder
Strategic Prayer Apostolic Network

I have had the privilege of knowing Tom Schlueter for about 15 years and have watched the growth and development of both Tom as an apostolic-prophetic leader, and that of the TXAPN. The strategic nature, and the honor demonstrated among the various ministries across Texas, with which Tom and TXAPN have worked with prophetic words, assignments, and divine opportunities serves a model to both challenge and encourage all who desire to see their cities, states, and nations move forward in the purposes of God.

The truths, principles, and process that Tom Schlueter communicates in his latest books present a valuable tool for anyone seeking to strategically advance the Kingdom of God where you live. Tom chronicles his own journey, along with that of the network that he partners with in such a way that it is certain to awaken ideas, strategies, and hope in the hearts of Kingdom advancers near and far.

Dive in and glean all that God has for you within these pages, then go forward in faith to do all God reveals to you. For His Glory!

Jacquie Tyre, Apostle
Jacquie Tyre Ministries
www.jacquietyre.com

As I write the endorsement for this book of testimony, I reach deep into the heart of God and take hold of a seed word called "covenant". As you read the stories and the glories, you are reading a line of covenant testimony. I begin and end this endorsement honoring my friend, Apostle Tom Schlueter, for the courage to seek a covenant understanding – not so much for theological fact but to LIVE it. He so richly begins by saying, "This is not a "how". This is a "Who". I pray many leaders read this book as a leader's manual as well as an inspiration of what God can do when we honor relationship.

As you read the beginnings to the end, folded into these stories are droughts that ended, lakes and rivers healed of pollution, cities turned upside down, righteous leaders coming into place and miracles only God could do. Also folded in are stories of people that came together for the glory of God. Many have their ministry titles, their ministries, their histories but those all were laid down for the greater quest of the Kingdom. We were melted together into an axe head through one experience after another with a song of joy unspeakable.

Now, I again, sincerely honor, Tom and Kay Schlueter, for the seriously great courage it takes to lead like this. They forsook their own often. They joined in the honor of others and the advancement of others for the good of the whole. I have observed them trust God through what could be confusion, pain and much else but look at this axe-head called Texas that shines for Jesus alone!

Enjoy the stories but especially glean from what God can do when we yield to become what He is going to wield in this nation!

Merrie Cardin, Apostle
Brazos Covenant Ministries, Granbury, Texas
TXAPN Lead Apostolic Council and Rolling Plains Coordinator

It has been my honor and privilege to walk in ministry and covenant friendship with Tom Schlueter since 2007. Tom has the "patience of Job" and the determination of Paul. He is a trusted leader. By the grace of God, my 40 plus years of full-time ministry has been filled with "running the race" with forerunners and pioneers. In 2007, Texas Apostolic Prayer Network was birthed and once again I found myself on the leadership team of a forerunner ministry. TXAPN was and is bringing unprecedented relational connection, prophetic revelation and apostolic direction to the intercessory prayer movement in Texas. We have not "arrived" but the ministry of TXAPN has become more of a movement than just a ministry. The movement is now emerging as a model that can inspire and empower intercessors and leaders across our nation. Tom Schlueters book **Wielding The Axe** is full of prophetic testimony, revelation, practical explanation and undeniable results. This book is must reading!

Bob Long, Apostle
TXAPN Lead Apostolic Council and Capital Region Coordinator
Apostolic Founder/Overseer: Rally Call Ministries
and Rally Call Leadership (www.rallycall.net)
Former Director Of New Testament Leadership Studies at
Christ For The Nations Institute

It is a tangible thing to live in the presence of God's reality! This work, within these pages is summarized in Ephesians 2:6 and verse 10. *"He raised us up with Christ the exalted One, and we ascended with Him into the glorious perfection and authority of the heavenly realm, for we are now co-seated as one with Christ! (v.10) We have become His poetry, a re-created people that will fulfill the destiny He has given each of us, for we are joined to Jesus, the Anointed One. Even before we were born, God planned in advance our destiny and the good works we would do to fulfill it!"* (TPT)

Sit before His Majesty in Heaven as you allow Him to navigate your journey through this book. This Covenant Team, TXAPN continues to marvel at His tangible poetry within these vessels of clay! The "emphatic" is Jesus! We are attracted to Him, then His Presence within us expresses His commanding authority on earth as in Heaven. Your family, your community, your sphere of influence is waiting for "His commanding authority" to be known through you. Give Jesus permission to take Tom and Kay's journey and the journey of TXAPN deep into your reality so that His refining work explodes in Heavenly poetry!

Hollis and Carol Jean Kirkpatrick
Servants To The City
TXAPN Trinity Region Coordinators

Wielding the Axe

A MODEL TO BOTH CHALLENGE AND TO ENCOURAGE US TO MOVE FORWARD WITH THE PURPOSES OF GOD

Dr. Thomas Schlueter

DEDICATION

First, I dedicate this book to my loving wife, Kay. For over 46 years she has loved me, supported me, challenged me, corrected me and "gotten in my face," because that's what family does. I could not have done this and will not be able to continue to do this, without her help. And by the way, she makes the best jam in Texas and you can check out Jammin' Nana at www.texasapn.com.

This book is also dedicated to the grassroots warriors of the Ekklesia in Texas. I especially honor the members of the Texas Apostolic Prayer Network Council. They are:

Lonnie and Rhonda Brooks, Penny Simmons, Mark Wauahdooah, Eddie and Merrie Cardin, Laura Mallory, Mary Ann Tittsworth, Anne Tate, Jorge Lorenzana, Hollis and Carol Jean Kirkpatrick, Peggy Connett, Laura Terrell, Joyce Shaver, Dianne Young, Linda Dennis, Kristy Edwards, Trayce Bradford, Donna Craig, Ken and Ginny Bryan, Gary and RaJean Vawter, Kerry and Diane Kirkwood, Fred and Carmen Johnson, Mark Portugal, Don and Pat Palmer, Donna Kelly, Jimmy and Martha Dusek, Fritz and Debra Rosenthal, Kat Rowoldt, Michael and Christy Maris, Gilda Wilkinson, Kim Ulmer, Patsy Chmelar, Cody and Cheri Clemmons, Robin Durham, Emma Colbert, Betty Johnson, Nancy Nicholson, Frank and Yesenia Jones, Debbie Burk, Bob Long, Cynthia Griffith, Cody and Rene'e Haynes, Kerry and Toni Hellums, Mary Bostrom, Christine George, Betty Huff, Neal and Darla Ryden, Amanda Rossy, Jennifer Meyer, Jenalee Alexander, Olivia Mohle, Taylor Kilponen, Sharon Denney, Theresa Estrada, Jeremy and Tandy Burk, Wanda Ulrey, Linda Goodwin, Laura Reeves, Loretta Brown, Gary and Patricia Wilhite, Esther Gallegos, Frank and Ruby Dodson, Chris and Dorothy Dundas.

And finally, I dedicate this to the Lord of my life. He is my King, my savior, my friend and the One whom I will eternally serve. Thank you Jesus, that you trusted us to steward in prayer the state of Texas and this nation.

WIELDING THE AXE

ACKNOWLEDGEMENTS

I must acknowledge my Dad and Mom, Rev. Arnold and Helen Schlueter. Earlier in this year of 2020 they celebrated 75 years of marriage and ministry. Mom passed into heaven's glory in August and Dad celebrated his 99th birthday in September. They taught me to pray. They have been my most ardent supporters and mentors.

I wish to acknowledge Chuck Pierce, Dutch Sheets, Cindy Jacobs and Jim Hodges who exemplify the meaning of apostolic and prophetic leadership and mentorship. They have been my strongest allies and encouragers. I thank the Lord that I am in covenant with them.

I acknowledge the wonderful Ekklesia that meets as Prince of Peace House of Prayer and how they have grasped ahold of their destiny and calling in God's Kingdom. They worship through a God-ordained portal. They are family!

I cannot express with words the covenantal love I share with the **Elders at the Gate**: Jon Bunn, Burton Purvis, Hollis Kirkpatrick, Sam Dewald, Chris Shields and Jorge Lorenzana.

And thank you David Munoz for the beautiful and powerful cover!

The Lord would say, "Texas, you are My battle axe. You are My shield."

The Lord said, "I am pouring out My Spirit upon you to protect the nation. I am pouring out the spirit of a warrior upon TXAPN. Gird your loins, be strong, because I have you on the forefront; you are frontline. You are on the battlefront. I am not having you at the back of the battle, you are on the front of the battle. Your prayers are availing much. This state will be on fire for the gospel. I am getting ready to light gospel fires that are going to spring up in so many little places."

The Lord shows me all these rural places that the fire of God is going to hit. It is not just going to hit in the cities. The fire of God will come to Austin, and even to the city of Dallas, the city of Houston, not just the outskirts.

The Lord says, "Look to the rural communities, for I am going to pour out like a Cane Ridge Revival with the fear of the Lord. And I going to raise up evangelists that are going to have such an anointing upon what they say, that people will fall under the power of God, and the fear of the Lord will grip them, just as in days of yore."

Prophet Cindy Jacobs
July 28, 2020

TABLE OF CONTENTS

FOREWORDS

It has been my great honor to be part of the prayer movement in America for 30 plus years. In that span of time, I've been blessed with a front row seat from which I could watch it evolve and mature. During this same time period, I have also participated in and observed the restoration of Christ's prophetic anointing to the church, followed by that of the apostolic. Over time, it became clear to me that Holy Spirit was braiding these movements into a powerful 3-fold cord, which would be used by Him as a mighty force to change the world.

Though no movement can claim perfection or full maturity—we will be forever growing in our understanding of God and His ways—nevertheless, Holy Spirit has matured and coalesced these three movements into a powerful collective force. I am often filled with excitement in corporate gatherings of prayer and worship as I observe the high level of wisdom and revelation being demonstrated. God has indeed, on a worldwide level, raised up a powerful army and a mature governing force, which is quite possibly unequaled in history. In short, the ekklesia, of which Jesus said the gates of hell would not prevail against (Matthew 16:18-19), has now emerged.

After an institution or coalition is formed, however, further growth and development is always needed. The same is true spiritually. That which has been learned in the head and heart must grow in its ability to be applied. Spiritual transformation is not an exact science. Mistakes will undoubtably occur, adjustments will need to be made, and procedures will evolve. That's when the experience of forerunners like Tom Schlueter and TXAPN become so valuable.

As I have observed and worked with Tom over the last several years, I've witnessed the following pattern: 1) he listens carefully to Holy Spirit's instructions; 2) he then faithfully obeys and diligently applies the instructions; and 3) this process produces greater wisdom, understanding, and ability with which to lead in the future at an even higher level. Though Tom would never claim to have done everything perfectly, I've watched him build and lead one of the most effective kingdom endeavors in the nation. So effective, in fact, that leaders from around the nation are now beginning to ask for his help in their regions, realizing that the transformational principles implemented in Texas have created a path others can follow. Tom, and the ekklesia Christ has assembled in Texas, have become forerunners, blazing a trail for all of us. The purpose of this book is to mark that trail.

This roadmap does not consist of formulas and methods. When the formularizing of spiritual truth is attempted, religion and tradition rear their ugly heads, choking the life out of that which once pulsated with power and vitality. However, when Holy Spirit's acts and instructions are not methodized, much wisdom can be imparted to those who have ears to hear. That is the purpose of this book.

As I have observed regional transformation from within the movement, a few patterns and "non-negotiables" have emerged among the efforts of the successful:

- Apostolic, prophetic, kingdom-minded leaders (those who care more about the advancement of Christ's cause than the success of their individual ministries) must be at the forefront. Both of these ministry gifts are essential and must work together—neither can succeed without the other. This team must be led by an apostolic point person, who has the time, desire, anointing, and calling to do so as their primary kingdom responsibility. If he or she sees the role as a secondary assignment, the effort will fail.
- The apostolic and prophetic anointings must be infused into all prayer and activity. Holy Spirit's instruction and strategy must first be heard (the prophetic) and prioritized. Far too often ministries and organizations endeavor to impact regions through good ideas and programs. However, formulas do not succeed in the application of spiritual truth; only hearing and obeying will produce results. While I would never imply that we shouldn't use our intellect and logic, I would nonetheless emphasize that this can never replace the word of the Lord, which reveals correct timing, prayer targets, effective strategies, strongholds of the enemy, and more. Also, however, the insights and strategies of Holy Spirit must be implemented (the apostolic). As obvious as this seems, it is often where failure lies. Countless times I have heard the word of the Lord released to a person or region, yet no action was ever taken. Without coordination and implementation, no breakthrough will occur. Boots must hit the ground—prayer journeys, unified decrees, corporate fasts, worship and prayer gatherings, and more must occur. These activities require apostolic order and oversight.
- Lastly, a willing network of committed, kingdom-minded intercessors must be "recruited" and aligned with the apostolic/prophetic leadership Holy Spirit forms. A team must form—a willing team, an army. This requires time, effort, coordination, money, and the right leader.

Where these conditions are met, success is seen. Unfortunately, there are only a few states or regions in the United States where all of these attributes are working together at a high level. Under Tom's leadership, Texas is one of them. Thanks to books like this, more will follow.

If you are a regional leader whom God is raising up to lead in your area, read this book to discover the principles applied by Tom and the TXAPN. Then, ask Holy Spirit how to apply them in your region. If you're a member of a team, do the same, but with a heart to serve the leader/s. If we faithfully do our part, Holy Spirit will certainly do His. And please believe me when I say: where the plans and purposes of Christ and His kingdom on earth are concerned...the best is yet to come!

Dutch Sheets, Apostle
Dutch Sheets Ministries
National Ekklesia International Director

I am so excited about the words Tom Schlueter has written upon the pages of "Wielding the Axe." Tom, out of his years of faithful pursuit of God's design for warfare that brings victory, has laid out a very clear and needed strategy for our future. His experiences have shaped and molded this man of God into a General of strategy. The reading of this book is like stepping into a Citadel. It positions you in a lofted place to be observant of the battles that rage but gives you a bird's eye view of how to be postured for victory. Ecclesiastes 10:10 states "If the axe is dull, and one does not sharpen the edge, then he must use more strength; but wisdom brings success." (NKJV) Many know how to wield the axe they have been given but fail to take the significant time essential to keep the edge sharpened. Without that sharpened edge they become weary through the need of added strength and lose their cutting edge, eventually walking away. Tom's way of sharing the wisdom he has gained through keeping his edge sharp will become the whetstone and oil needed to attain your fine edge. Thank you, Tom, for this endeavor and the life and intentional focus it will bring to many. You, yes you, are called to rule, and "Wielding the Axe" will certainly prove to be a resource you will return to many times, just as I have with "Could you not Tarry One Hour."

Clay Nash, Apostle
Author of <u>Activating the Prophetic</u>, <u>Relational Authority</u> and <u>God Dreams To Make America Great Again</u>
Network Ekklesia International leader
ClayNash.org

PREFACE

In the fall of 1988, I arrived here at Arlington, Texas and began my ministry at Prince of Peace Lutheran Church. I remember reviewing the beginning of this ministry with great anticipation and excitement. Before moving to Arlington, I had been working on my doctorate at Fuller Theological Seminary in church growth. Here was a small congregation ready to move with the Holy Spirit and ready to grow. It was a good season.

I don't have time to write a complete story of what happened over the next few years but let it suffice to say that God had other plans then the ones that I proposed. He made it very clear to me, after one very vigorous spiritual temper tantrum (I've had several of these), that He did not bring me here to grow a church, but to manifest His kingdom. Even as a Spirit filled Lutheran pastor, I had no idea what He meant. He continued to reveal to me that this would be a house of prayer, but I had my own ideas and understanding about what a house of prayer would look like. And once again, after a tantrum, he revealed to me that Prince of Peace would be a strategic House of prayer.

I remember one moment in my personal prayer life with the Lord, that I complained that the members of the church we're not even embracing the prayer programs that I was initiating so how were they going to be a strategic house of prayer. And what does "strategic "mean? The Lord answered back, "they're just not praying the way you want them to." He also informed that this "house of prayer" was not to be modeled after the revelation given to the leaders in Kansas City or other house of prayer movements. He was developing and releasing a "new thing." I realized that I had to learn some things about prayer that were not only going to be built on my previous experiences but were going to drastically change what prayer, and especially strategic prayer, was all about.

It's obvious in reference to my opening sentence that I grew up in the Lutheran Church, and my prayer life had been defined by the practices of Lutheranism. We depended on the Pastor, my dad, being the only one who would pray the church prayers on Sunday morning. We depended on the use of prayer books and devotionals to lead us through our times of prayer, both corporately and individually.

Many of those prayer books were founded on the written prayers of Martin Luther and other church fathers as well as the Book of Common Prayer.

> The <u>Book of Common Prayer</u> is the short title of a number of related prayer books used in the Anglican Communion, as well as by other Christian churches historically related to Anglicanism. The original book, published in 1549 in the reign of Edward VI, was a product of the English Reformation following the break with Rome. The work of 1549 was the first prayer book to include the complete forms of service for daily and Sunday worship in English. It contained Morning Prayer, Evening Prayer, the Litany, and Holy Communion and also the occasional services in full: the orders for Baptism, Confirmation, Marriage, "prayers to be said with the sick", and a funeral service. It also set out in full the "Propers" (the parts of the service which varied week by week or, at times, daily throughout the Church's Year): the introits, collects, and epistle and gospel readings for the Sunday service of Holy Communion. Old Testament and New Testament readings for daily prayer were specified in tabular format as were the Psalms; and canticles, mostly biblical, that were provided to be said or sung between the readings.[1]

I began to realize that my prayer life was based solely on reading or reciting prayers found in prayer books, or in the simple prayers a child would pray at bedtime and mealtime. The Lord would start me on a journey that would lead me towards a spiritual walk of uncommon prayer. Let me state that what looks uncommon is not. As I write this book, I am not wanting to express deep theological premises and systematic doctrines. This book is not meant to be a thorough instruction regarding God's presence or prayer. I desire to present, in a simple way, the principles I have learned, not only of prayer, but of a life in Him which have laid a foundation for a statewide network of prayer. I invite you to step into this journey with me. It is meant to be a "primer" which hopefully will ignite in each reader an awareness of what the Lord has intended from the beginning to be planted in each one of His created children. "Lord, there is a pilot light burning in each of us. Turn up the thermostat and let the full fire of Your presence burn in us. Amen."

Dr. Thomas Schlueter

---

[1] Wikipedia contributors. (2018, November 23). Book of Common Prayer. In *Wikipedia, The Free Encyclopedia*. Retrieved 15:40, November 27, 2018, from https://en.wikipedia.org/w/index.php?title=Book_of_Common_Prayer&oldid=870186222

PROLOGUE

What's the purpose of this book? As I wrote my two previous books, <u>Return of the Priests</u> and <u>Keeper of the Keys</u>,[2] I was asked by my editors, "What is the purpose of the book? Who's the audience? What do you want them to hear?" In answering those questions, I could easily acknowledge that the audience was very wide open and general. There were many in the church that needed to hear and read about who they were in Christ Jesus and the authority that they carry in carrying out the work of his Kingdom.

But that is not this book. Several years ago, when I was teaching some intercessors about the assignments of prayer that we carry out, I used the following analogy of hitting the target. In years past many of our prayers were like the bombings that took place in Europe during World War II. The bomb bay doors were opened, and hundreds of bombs fell on the ground below – hoping to hit the target. Then we saw the strategy change in Desert Storm. We watched on our televisions in amazement as GPS coordinates carried a missile to a very specific spot, and the target was demolished.

This book is meant for some very specific targets.

- It's directed towards those who would provide leadership for intercessory prayer in a home, local church, a city, a county, a state or a nation.
- It is meant for those who have received that "call" from God to get on the front lines of authoritative and declaratory prayer.
- It is intended for those who no longer will do it "themselves" but will seek out the synergy of covenant relationships.
- It is aimed at the sons and daughters of the Most High God who are willingly and passionately pursuing Him and His purposes.

Obviously, that includes all of those who are reading this. We can no longer follow old models. We can no longer embrace a task of providing coordinated leadership by depending on one individual or even a small team. Let me make an important note here that there is a place for small covert teams which will go out to "spy out the land" and carry out specific assignments. But a grassroots army must be lifted up. So, if you are an intercessor and especially a prayer leader of a small group of prayer warriors in your home, your local church, a city or a county or a state, I'm writing to you. Yes, I will be sharing the story of Texas, but this can be your story as well.

---

[2] Both of these books are available in Kindle and Paperback through Amazon

INTRODUCTION

I have been and continue to carry out a role as an apostolic leader in the state of Texas. My role includes being a coordinator at a national level with other states. Several years ago, the Lord gave me a word, "The strength of a nation is in the power of the individual states."

Interestingly, that is the very essence of who we are as a nation. We are not to see a federal government that oversees the states with unrelenting power and authority. The power of our nation is with the people and in the individual strength and giftings of each of the states. The same is true for any initiatives of prayer. I hope to lay out in the following pages a short but succinct message that you must hear what God is saying to you regarding your home, your church, your city, your county, or your state. Research where you live. Discover the giftings and the destiny of your assignment. Read books like <u>Releasing The Prophetic Destiny of the Nation: Discovering How Your Future Can Be Greater Than Your Past </u>by Chuck Pierce and Dutch Sheets.[3]

But most importantly, seek the face of the Lord and listen for His directions as you partner with God in His creation of a grassroots movement across the nation. Our nation's destiny is at stake and we can no longer depend on a few anointed leaders to carry out the task. God is raising up an army and you are enlisted, by His Spirit and calling, into that army. Over the years, as a network of intercessors has been developing across the state of Texas, many have asked me, "How did you do it?" I sensed in their query that they were looking for some sort of a formula or a strategy that could be used in their own situation, whether that be in a city, a county or a state. Some were merely wanting to hear a testimony. As you read the following pages, this is not a "how to" book. You will read about revelations that the Lord gave us regarding our assignments in the state. **The gathering and networking of intercessors happened as we obediently carried out what the Lord had assigned us to do.**

It all began in January of 2007, before the network existed, when I heard the Lord speak to me. He commanded me to drive the circumference of the state of Texas and honestly, I wasn't sure of the purpose of that trip. But I said "yes." Little did I know that five months later I would be asked to lead a new network of intercessors for the state. And after I was commissioned in the state capital of Texas by Chuck Pierce in June of that year, my wife Kay and I started our trek. I

---

[3] Published in 2005 by Destiny Image. Available through Amazon

had sent out an email to approximately three hundred people that I had as contacts for around the Dallas-Fort Worth area and across the state. As we started our journey, many of them asked if they could join us along the way by providing a meal or a place to stay, *and the network was birthed.* It wasn't my strategy. It was simply obeying the Lord's command. As we obediently carried out His wishes, He added to us, not only numbers, but more importantly strategies, assignments and initiatives that were meant to release His Kingdom in and through the State of Texas.

I encourage you to read our story. Don't look for a formula. Look for Him – our Lord and King. Carry out what He commands you to do. No more delay. He's forming His Ekklesia into a mighty army.

And don't forget to eat. I have a reputation on Facebook for the posting of the many meals that I have eaten across the state. Of course, I'm in search for the best hamburger, the best chicken fried steak, the best steak and many other delicacies. But I've made it very clear when people have asked me about those pictures, that I typically do not take a picture of food unless it is somehow attached with a meal that I am having with those that make up the grassroots of Texas. Just recently, we were having a meal with leaders from another state in Washington D.C. and we were commenting to them how important it was to take that time and to sit down together as brothers and sisters in Christ at a table and to share a meal together. It's not just about eating. It's about covenant. It's amazing the number of times the Lord sat down with His disciples to eat. You might be eating prime rib or a hamburger, but it is not the food that counts. It is the covenant fellowship of those that you are going to war with. It's about strengthening those relationships. It's about strategizing. It's about relaxing and having fun. It's about enjoying the work of the Kingdom.

Therefore, I must acknowledge that this book would mean nothing if it were not for the covenant brothers and sisters who have walked the walk together. This is not a one-man job. This is not a small team of state leaders doing all the work. This is literally an army. I cherish the coordinators from across the state that carry out the grassroots work of interceding and legislating on behalf of God's Kingdom. They must be acknowledged. They are the true warriors. One has said in the past, "If you are a leader and yet no one is behind you, you're simply taking a walk." I can testify that that is not the case, at every level, in the network and movement of prayer here in the state of Texas.

Tom Schlueter

1

SOMETHING NEW

Yahweh is the one who makes a way in the sea,
a pathway in the mighty waters.
He destroyed chariots and horses
and all their mighty warriors.
They fell, never to rise again—
gone forever, snuffed out like a wick. This is what he says "Stop
dwelling on the past.
Don't even remember these former things.
I am doing something brand new, something unheard of.
Even now it sprouts and grows and matures.
Don't you perceive it?
I will make a way in the wilderness
and open up flowing streams in the desert.
(Isaiah 43:16-19 The Passion Translation)

It was June of 2007 and over three hundred people gathered by divine appointment in the auditorium of the state capital of Texas. It was time for a new season. Apostle and Prophet Chuck Pierce had invited me, Tom Schlueter, to oversee the forming of a new prayer network in Texas. That invitation had arrived to me, interestingly, as I was visiting a World War II battlefield in Europe.

That night in Austin, Chuck presented me with a large key[4] and commissioned me to take leadership over the newly formed Texas Apostolic Prayer Network. I was expecting Chuck to then do a teaching, but instead, he handed me the microphone and said, "It's all yours." I was nervous and overwhelmed, but immediately received a word from the Lord. He declared through me, "I will use Texas to change and shift the nation, if you will deal with your two major strongholds - pride and independence." As a group we immediately went to our knees and repented.

---

[4] Keys are extremely important to me. My last name Schlueter is an occupational name derived from German and means "keeper of the keys of the prison." The Lord on certain assignments, too many to number, has asked me to open or close spiritual doors. You can read more in my book, <u>Keeper of the Keys</u> from Amazon.

I'm sharing this incident because as I unfold what the Lord has been doing in and through Texas over these last several decades, and specifically over the last 13 years with the Texas Apostolic Prayer Network (TXAPN), that you will hopefully receive it with no hint of pride or independence. We continue to humbly present ourselves before the Lord, asking him to use us as a network to carry out his commanded assignments of prayer throughout the state, but also into and throughout our nation.

It is imperative in this hour that all of us evaluate the assignments that the Lord has given us, and how he intends to use all of us, individually and corporately, to carry out his Kingdom mandates in order that we might see a transformation and an awakening in our nation that is never been seen before. He has literally lifted us up in Texas, not only to pray and intercede, but to go out with Him as an army to release His purposes and His destiny for Texas and the Nation.

A Visitation

Let me begin this journey by recounting an experience that I had in 2016. The following experience or visitation took place as I was on the flight back from Washington D.C. where I had attended a gathering of Native American leaders at the All Tribes DC gathering on October 21 of that year.

The first part refers back to a pair of dreams that I had had almost 30 years ago where the Lord made it clear that I was running ahead of him and moving in my own strategies. Those two dreams, that took place two nights in a row, literally changed the design, the strategy and the focus of my ministry.

The main part of what I'm sharing will reference a whirlwind or hurricane that I saw at the end of the visitation. I believe it confirms and ties together with Chuck Pierce's word regarding the wind being released that has been held in heaven for the last eight years (2008-2016).

I refer you also to a word that he gave to me earlier in 2016: "I am bringing my people out of Babylon." We are entering the season of restoration, victory and celebration.

With Jesus at 33,000 feet.

I was settled into my seat and ready for some "alone" time. I'm not one who visits with those seated around me. I wanted to rest or listen to music and read a book. All of a sudden, I felt carried away into another place.

It's been a long time but I'm once again walking with Jesus on the seashore of Galilee. We've been here before in previous dreams. I remember him stopping as I walked on. He was stooping down and picking up rocks - challenging me to come back to Him rather than journeying on alone. But this time I was the one who stopped. I was wanting to linger. I longed for more "still" time with Him. I was wanting to toss rocks in the water, but He was walking ahead. He turned to me and beckoned me to follow. He said to me...

"Don't linger. Don't wait. We have a great adventure ahead of us. I'm taking you to places you've never been. I'm walking with you into the great season of your life. Don't be afraid to let go of some things that you cherish. They have prepared you for this journey but come on - let's walk!"

As I walked, I saw a whole new set of armor being placed on me. I don't know how to describe it. It is brilliant in color. It glows as crystal or as diamonds but looks pure like gold. It is strong and impenetrable.
He said, "Wherever you walk you will strengthen the land. You will release light into the atmosphere no matter how dark. There is a troop with you. You are not alone. They are armored as you are for that has been your desire. We will walk together. My kingdom is here. My will is done."

He is embracing me, and all of His life force is encompassing me. Not only am I feeling strength, passion and newness but all infirmity is melting away. I breath it out from me. I speak it into the atmosphere. Holy. Beautiful. Whole. I'm supposed to commune with Him. Even as I was in this place of visitation, He allowed me to physically take communion.

I communed on the plane by eating cookies. Beautiful food. "Taste and see that the Lord is good (beautiful)." "Taste and see that the LORD is good. Oh, the joys of those who take refuge in him! Fear the LORD, you his godly people, for those who fear him will have all they need. Even strong young lions sometimes go hungry, but those who trust in the LORD will lack no good thing" (Psalm 34:8-10 NLT).

I drank red wine which the flight attendant gave to me with no cost. "Come and eat. Come and drink with no cost. Is anyone thirsty? Come and drink— even if you have no money! Come, take your choice of wine or milk— it's all free" (Isaiah 55:1 New Living Translation)!

As I ate and drank, I felt impurities leaving me. It is His body. It is His blood. He strengthened and cleansed me. As we walked on in the visitation, we walked up an incline as though on steps but there is no

exertion on my part. With each step I feel more strength. I briefly look nostalgically behind me. He smiles at me knowing that what was behind me has disappeared. It is not gone from my memory, for it had set the stage, but it now disappeared for it no longer is my story. The story is being written as we walk. A new chapter with each step. Each step is a victory.
Each step I feel something hitting me. It seems as though they are arrows or spears, but they do not prosper against me. I see trials and turbulence around me, but the weapons vanish as Jesus and the troop with me walk on. He declares, "Every step you take is a possession of the Kingdom being taken away from the enemy."

I notice for the first time that we are surrounded by a host of angel warriors. They have always been there, and they will walk with us. We are together like a whirlwind, a hurricane of God's glory and presence moving across the land. This is overwhelming! O Lord Jesus! What was so amazing about this time with Him was this. We walked together. We grasped each other's hand. I felt His arm around me. "Thank you, Jesus. I love you!" Later as I revisited this visitation, I realized that we were in the eye of the storm and literally, with Jesus, a part of the storm. The wind and we are as one.

Here is Chuck Pierce's word that I referenced earlier.

> *"For the last eight years I have been blowing winds in the heavens. Winds have been stirring and stirring and stirring in My heavens. But now those winds are released to come into the earth realm. What has been stirring in Heaven will now blow in the earth. Brace yourself! Brace yourself! Brace yourself! Brace yourself! For the winds that will now blow are the winds I've been holding back over the last eight years. Because I've been holding them back and you've been asking for them to blow earlier, <u>NOW</u> I will release them. I am acting on how you have sought Me in the last eight years.*
>
> *"These winds will begin to gather an army of those that have been faithful and those that will now gather into a place they didn't even know they belonged. The winds of adversity will now produce an army (of whom) people will say, 'It is the LORD's army that has changed the course of history!' Tonight, and beginning this week, you will be bringing the turning point winds into the earth and rearranging the course of what is to become. Nations will begin now in their realignment with other nations, but I will blow off the façade that has been holding you captive. Because you have gathered here in this turning point*

> *state, now the turning point winds[5] will come. What I've held back for eight years, I must now release. What goes on through May (as you begin to honor Me, and walk with Me, and gather with Me) will create a nation that has been covered over by the enemy's hand. The winds that now blow in the earth will cause the hand of the enemy that has been controlling the movement of strategy in the earth in this nation to be seen. No longer will the enemy have an upper hand in this land!"[6]*

The two dreams that I experienced those many years ago literally caused my ministry and my life in the Lord to make a dramatic turn. And so was the case with this visitation at 33,000 feet. The Lord is taking us into new places. He has opened the door to a new era of His glory. He is providing us weapons and the assistance of angelic forces that we've never experienced before that will release, through us, a manifestation of His Kingdom in the spheres of influence that we occupy.

Over the last several months and years, the Lord has been speaking to me that He is disrobing me. He is taking off old structures, old mindsets, old paradigms, and old ideas that we have depended upon for many, many years in carrying out the work of the church. He came to me a few weeks ago and declared very clearly, "I'm tired of the best laid plans of mice and men." This is a season for new armor, new anointings, new strength and new strategies. We must embrace what he is doing with us now. He is drawing us into a place of intimate fellowship – communion with him – in order to bring forth a revelation to us of what we need to be doing in this season that has never been done before. This is a season, like never before, that we need to pay very close attention to the revelations that he releases to us.

And He is not going to permit us to do it by ourselves. Here in Texas, we have thoroughly researched and embraced the redemptive gift of the state. The redemptive gifts are based on the Father gifts in Romans 12:3-8 which have been taught by Arthur Burk and others. The best book on the gifts is by my friend, Ruthie Young, and is entitled: <u>Your Destiny, His Glory! The How and Why of Your Design</u>.[7] Over the years, the Lord made it very clear that the redemptive gift of Texas is "Prophet." One of the traits of this gift is to go "out front" as a visionary. The prophet sees ahead. Now I do not intend to teach on this gift right now, but that one aspect of "going ahead" fits the spiritual DNA of Texas.

---

[5] The theme of the turning point or the tide is turning has been very prevalent in the revelations the Lord has been giving me for the last year or so. I will write more on it in the following pages.
[6] Chuck Pierce, Given in May of 2016
[7] Ruthie Young's book is available on Amazon.

But we also discovered that this prophet gift can try to work independent of others and "leave the others behind." That will not work in God's order and design. In order for this gift of prophet to be truly redemptive, the prophet gift must embrace the concept of covenant. We must move ahead and work together – utilizing all the other six redemptive gifts. We need the grassroots. As you will discover in the revelations and prophecies I'll share throughout the book, the Lord will continually speak of our calling to take the lead, but always in the context of working together. As I mentioned earlier, He told us: "I will use Texas to change and shift the nation, if you will deal with your two major strongholds – pride and independence."

He is causing a synchronization and a synergy to take place as He covenantally ties us together with each other to carry out what we thought we could do by ourselves in years past. As Dutch Sheets has proclaimed, "God is revealing the synergy of the ages." He is drawing on all the prayers of the past and all the anointings of powerful intercessors of the past. He is collecting the cries of prayer in past generations, and He is bringing them all into a place where we will explode exponentially with the revelations and power of God.

2

The Dream

With her enticing speech she caused him to yield,
With her flattering lips she seduced him.
Immediately he went after her, as an ox goes to the slaughter,
Or as a fool to the correction of the stocks.
(Proverbs 7:21-22 New King James Version)

It was Friday, September 4th of 2020. My wife, Kay, and I we're making our way to San Antonio to celebrate my dad's 99th birthday. We had just attended an evening and a morning of a very strategic season of authoritative prayer regarding our nation as it approaches this crucial election.

After a great supper and settling in for the night, I was invaded early in the morning with a very vivid and troubling dream. In the dream a former elder of my congregation, I will call him Hank, was aggressively seducing my wife. He was persistent. He tried every angle. I was getting disturbed and upset in the dream, and I was taking a position of protection with my wife. I commanded him many times to leave the room. But he was persistent. I felt as though the seduction might work but I continued to press against him. As the dream ended, I woke up with a panic. My body was shaking. I was angry. I told a friend of mine later that day that if that person had been in our hotel room when I woke up, and if I had had a gun, he would have been sent to heaven. I knew the dream was very symbolic and didn't refer directly to that person or to my wife, but I was still very troubled. After spending a great deal of time just processing it without an answer, I went back to bed and slept very restlessly the rest of the morning. After getting ready the next day I did my normal pattern of reading the scriptures, morning prayers and a morning prayer call with Texas intercessors. After the prayer, I asked the Lord the meaning of the dream. He very clearly informed me that he wanted me to understand and feel the passionate anger that He has towards anyone that tries to seduce His bride, the church.

I realized, through the dream, that the Lord was highlighting those that were seducing his bride from inside the church. That is why there was an emphasis on an elder of the church. Though we are being attacked from all sides by the society that we are now living in, the emphasis of this dream was placed solely on the seduction of the church by those who are meant to lead it, oversee it, mentor it, and bring it forth into its destiny.

The church has been seduced. The bride has been attacked from both the outside, and sadly, from the inside. When those who are called to serve in the military of the United States take an oath, they declare the following: "I, [name], do solemnly swear that I will support and defend the Constitution of the United States against all enemies, *foreign and domestic*; that I will bear true faith and allegiance to the same; that I take this obligation freely, without any mental reservation or purpose of evasion; and that I will faithfully discharge the duties of the office on which I am about to enter. So help me God."[8] This oath is for an indeterminate period; no duration is specifically defined.

Even though we do not use this oath in the church, we do profess and confess our faith in the one true Lord and God of our lives, Jesus Christ. We commit ourselves to be His disciples. We swear allegiance to Him and to the gospel of His Kingdom. We are to faithfully carry out His Word – both written and revealed. Read carefully what Rev. Robert Hunt declared when they arrived on the shores at Cape Henry. This is a prayer that decrees the depth of commitment they had to their Lord. In 1607, they planted a cross on the shore, and he decreed:

> "We do hereby Dedicate this Land, and ourselves, to reach the People within these shores with the Gospel of Jesus Christ, and to raise up Godly generations after us, and with these generations take the Kingdom of God to all the earth. May this Covenant of Dedication remain to all generations, as long as this earth remains, and may this Land, along with England, be Evangelist to the World. May all who see this Cross, remember what we have done here, and may those who come here to inhabit join is in this Covenant..."

The majority of the evangelical churches of our nation have been wooed by a political and religious spirit. They have been seduced. In another familiar phrase, "they drank the Kool-Aid" which refers to those who were seduced and deceived unto death under the false teaching of Jim Jones. We have found it advantageous to buy into the social agenda of the culture. We are more concerned about attendance figures and offerings then we are about the holiness, faith and purity of

---

[8] (Title 10, US Code; Act of 5 May 1960 replacing the wording first adopted in 1789, with amendment effective 5 October 1962). Emphasis mine

the flock. Biblical principles have been hijacked. Dietrich Bonhoeffer wrote in <u>The Cost of Discipleship</u> that "Cheap grace is the grace we bestow on ourselves. Cheap grace is the preaching of forgiveness without requiring repentance, baptism without church discipline, Communion without confession...Cheap grace is grace without discipleship, grace without the cross, grace without Jesus Christ, living and incarnate."[9] We have abandoned Biblical morality and holiness.

These are grievous errors and sins that we have openly welcomed into our churches. But as I meditated on the dream over the next several days, *I felt that one of the primary seductions that the Lord was highlighting in my own heart regarded the "impotence" of the church to act as a manifestation of God's presence, glory, grace, compassion, power and authority that He has given us to be a change agent - an influence - in society to bring society and culture into alignment with His kingdom.*

The Lord has granted His church an authority that has been lying dormant. I was with a group of pastors that I'm in covenant, and I recalled to my memory a favorite scene from the animated Disney movie <u>Lion King</u>. In one scene, the young Simba and Nala are in the wrong place. They have disobeyed orders and they are now in the elephant graveyard. They are surrounded by hyenas and there is no escape. Simba roars but all that comes out is a meow. The hyenas laugh and jeer asking if that's all he's got. "Do it again they cry." He roars again but this time there is the mighty roar of a mighty lion as Mufasa, his father, stands behind him and the hyenas scatter. We should have the roar of a lion, but we whimper like a young house cat. That is not our position in Christ.

---

[9] Dietrich Bonhoeffer, <u>The Cost of Discipleship</u>, MacMillan Publishing, 1963. Page 47

3

Priests and Kings – A Call to the Common Person

And you shall be to Me a kingdom of priests and a holy nation.'
These are the words which you shall speak to the children of Israel."
(Exodus 19:6 New King James Version)

Grace to you and peace from Him who is and who was and who is to come, and from the seven Spirits who are before His throne, and from Jesus Christ, the faithful witness, the firstborn from the dead, and the ruler over the kings of the earth. To Him who loved us and washed us from our sins in His own blood, and has made us kings and priests to His God and Father,
to Him be glory and dominion forever and ever. Amen.
(Revelation 1:4-6 New King James Version)

Over the last 20 years or so the primary message that the Lord has had me teach and preach refers to the role that we have as sons and daughters of the Most High God. In Christ Jesus, we are kings and priests in the world in which we live. The priestly role that we carry out is where we draw near to our God with worship, prayer and fellowship. Our kingly role flows from that intimate relationship and releases God's presence and purpose into government, education, business, media, the arts, entertainment and the family.

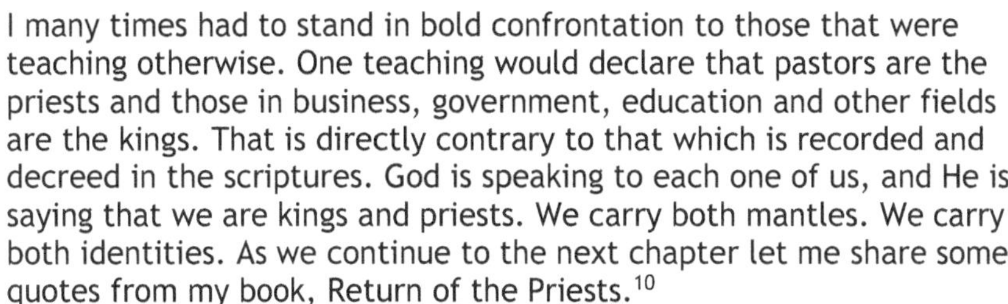

I many times had to stand in bold confrontation to those that were teaching otherwise. One teaching would declare that pastors are the priests and those in business, government, education and other fields are the kings. That is directly contrary to that which is recorded and decreed in the scriptures. God is speaking to each one of us, and He is saying that we are kings and priests. We carry both mantles. We carry both identities. As we continue to the next chapter let me share some quotes from my book, Return of the Priests.[10]

The priesthood is a call initiated and defined by God. It is a call based on our covenant relationship of faith and is an invitation

---

[10] You can order this book from Amazon in either paperback or Kindle format

into an intimate fellowship with God. The priesthood is carried out – not in the framework of a religious system – but in our everyday lives. The priesthood includes <u>all</u> people called, claimed and redeemed by God's sovereign will and grace through Jesus Christ. The priesthood is defined by an authority we are given to serve in God's kingdom in response to our intimate relationship with Him.[11]

Let's highlight one of those phrases. "…the priesthood includes all people called, claimed and redeemed by God's sovereign will and grace through Jesus Christ." God desires everyone to be a priest. Everyone is called into the intimacy of the throne room of God.[12] This is the priesthood of all believers.

As priests, we come to His heart. We discover, from His heart, what God wants us to release into the world, and then, with God-given authority, we take the message and work of God into the world as His priests. And on the other hand, we can also take the needs of those around us and carry them, as priests, before the throne of God, beseeching him to take care of their needs, to forgive their sins and to heal their diseases.

The church consists of corporate leaders, housewives, students, and teachers. They are young and old. Every single one of them is a priest. Every single one of them is defined as a child of God. And each of them could also be classified as a common everyday person. Few of them are well known in the world. Simple common people living common lives but called to an extraordinary destiny. God has called us into the priesthood and anointed us to come into His presence in order to release His authority into the world, in our workplace, in our neighborhood, in the places that we shop, in our schools, in our home, in government and wherever else the Lord might direct us.

Over the 40 plus years of ministry as a pastor, I have told people that the most common question I have been asked is this, "What is the call on their life?" I never was quite sure how I should answer them. But the Lord revealed to me that their call was to be a priest and a king. He literally told me that he was not as concerned about what their occupation was, but He was very committed in how they were carrying out their call through their occupation.

As I share those quotes from my book, I realize how many leaders in the church have seduced their members into believing that that is all

---

[11] Thomas Schlueter, <u>Return of the Priests</u>, Self-Published in 2004, Second Edition in 2017. page 17
[12] Ibid.

there is. And some leaders are not even willing to identify their members as priests. If you haven't been to Bible college, or if you haven't been to seminary, or if you haven't been taught how to lead in the church, then how could you possibly be a priest? But it is God who defines us. It is God who identifies us. It is God who calls us priests. Isn't it interesting that when the Lord is speaking to Israel in Exodus chapter 19[13] that he is speaking to the people of Israel? He is speaking to all of them. He is not just speaking to Moses and Aaron. He is speaking to all of His children gathered there at the mountain. **But then again, the seduction.** That's all you are. Your role is to help out in the local church or be sent to the mission field, but your priesthood is relegated or limited to the identity of that congregation in the community.

As I mentioned earlier, another seduction that is often taught within the church is that a priest is the person who carries out the role of prayer or leadership within the confines of the local church. But the king is the person who carries out the role of leadership in the world - in business, in government, in teaching, etc. That teaching is not supported through scripture. Each person is both a priest and a king. Let's look at some other quotes from my book, <u>Return of the Priest</u>. Let's look at the role of kings.

> We are priests. We are kings. We carry both mantles. We carry both identities. We are not just one and not the other. As sons and daughters of the highest God, we are kings and priests. God's Kingdom is a kingdom that will come as a kingdom of priests cry out to God, "Your Kingdom come; Your will be done on earth as it is in Heaven!"[14]
>
> God is waiting for us to usher in the Kingdom of God. He's waiting for us to stand up as a kingdom of priests and say, "Your Kingdom come; Your will be done on earth as it is in Heaven!" Declare it, saints! Speak it out, you priests! I entreat you. I beg you. God has empowered you as legislators

---

[13] Exodus 19:3-6: And Moses went up to God, and the LORD called to him from the mountain, saying, "Thus you shall say to the house of Jacob, and tell the children of Israel: 'You have seen what I did to the Egyptians, and *how* I bore you on eagles' wings and brought you to Myself. Now therefore, if you will indeed obey My voice and keep My covenant, then you shall be a special treasure to Me above all people; for all the earth *is* Mine. And you shall be to Me a kingdom of priests and a holy nation.' These *are* the words which you shall speak to the children of Israel." New King James Version®. Copyright © 1982 by Thomas Nelson. Used by permission. All rights reserved.

[14] Matthew 6:10. New King James Version®. Copyright © 1982 by Thomas Nelson. Used by permission. All rights reserved.

of His Kingdom to declare the kingdom of God in each of your spheres of influence – family, workplace, etc.[15]

If your home is your workplace, simply say first thing tomorrow morning, "God, let Your kingdom come and Your will be done in this place. As it is in Heaven, let it be on earth." Make the same declaration the next day and the next day and the next day. God is waiting for us to call on Him to reign in our homes. But it goes beyond our homes. In his book <u>The Gospel of the Kingdom,</u> George Eldon Ladd wrote this about the Lord's Prayer: "This prayer is a petition for God to reign, to manifest His kingly sovereignty and power, to put to flight every enemy of righteousness and of His divine truth that God alone may be king over all the world." [16]

I exhort you to declare "His kingdom come" in your workplace and to continue to say it until all unrighteousness begins to disappear.

"Lord, let Your kingdom reign in my life today. When I walk into the classroom, when I walk into my workplace, when I walk into the grocery store, while I'm cleaning or cooking; I want Your kingdom to come, Lord. I want Your will to be done." I believe that this has to be one of the most intense prayers that we offer to the point that we are willing to die to see God's Kingdom come into our circumstances. That is really the message of the martyrs. They were willing to die in order to see the kingdom of God manifested.[17]

When you study the Scriptures, you will see that the Kingdom of God is not referred to as a place. It's not referred to as a castle with a flag flying over it. God's Kingdom is always defined as God's rule and God's reign. Wherever God rules or reigns is His Kingdom. As we invite God to come and rule or reign in a place, that is where He will reign. Even when we don't invite Him, His rule is always going to overrule everything else because He is the One who lifts up and brings down kings and presidents. God is the One who orders the days. He's the One who sets the stars in place. God will rule and be sovereign no matter what, but as we invite Him, God's reign and rule will be released into and through our lives, and the very place we are standing will be transformed by His reign. It is important to understand that

---

[15] Thomas Schlueter, <u>Return of the Priests</u>, Self-Published in 2004, Second Edition in 2017. page 122

[16] George Eldon Ladd, *The Gospel of the Kingdom* (Grand Rapids, Michigan: Wm. B. Eerdmans Publishing Company, 1959), p. 21.

[17] Thomas Schlueter, <u>Return of the Priests</u>, Self-Published in 2004, Second Edition in 2017. page 123

when we are talking about God's Kingdom, we're not talking about a place. We're talking about His reign. When we say, "Lord, I want Your Kingdom to come," we are literally saying to Him:

> "Lord, You rule in my life. You set the standard. I am coming to You for my orders at the beginning of the day, the middle of the day and the end of the day because You are ruling my life - not I, but You. Rule and order my life in how I'm supposed to act, what I'm supposed to say, what I'm supposed to do, how I'm supposed to release Your Light into the world. You reign over me, Lord. Release Your reign over me."

> As God releases His reign over and through us, He will begin to transform the place where we are positioned as His priests. God will begin to establish His reign in our location, but His reign or His Kingdom is not defined by location. God is waiting for a royal priesthood, a holy nation, a kingdom of priests to invite Him to rule.[18]

It is extremely important that we grab ahold of and embrace this identity as a king. As I mentioned earlier, we have been deceived in thinking that that role is carried by those that are out there in government or in business. They are the ones that are making the ruling decisions. What is extremely frustrating is when I'm talking to someone who is in government or business, and they are trying their best to release the authority of God, but they're waiting for someone with a priestly role to help them. That is also a seduction. We are all priests and kings. We are all called into intimacy and we are all called to declare His rule and His reign. The institutional church is worshiping a false identity, not Jesus' identity. Ask the Lord to cut away the blinders, the webs and the deceptions that are keeping us, as the church, from fully embracing who we are in Jesus.

In 2011, I was trying with every effort to get an audience with the Governor of Texas. I sent letters. I talked to friends who had access to him. The doors would not open. I pleaded with the Lord, "there are things I feel the governor needs to declare over the state." The Lord answered me quickly, "you need to understand that you (Tom) have more authority than he does." His answer shook me. I stopped my efforts. I repented. The next week, the Lord opened the door to the Governor's office.

As we move into the next chapters, all that I have shared so far is the

---

[18] Thomas Schlueter, <u>Return of the Priests</u>, Self-Published in 2004, Second Edition in 2017. page 124

foundation that the Lord put into place as we began to carry out our role as intercessors and leaders, apostles and prophets in the state of Texas and the nation. Let me first describe the orders that He has given us as kings and priests in this hour.

4

The Vision and The Command

*The noise of a multitude in the mountains, like that of many people! A tumultuous noise of the kingdoms of nations gathered together! The Lord of hosts musters the **army** for battle.*
(Isaiah 13:4 New King James Version, emphasis added)

You will not need to fight in this battle. Position yourselves, stand still and see the salvation of the LORD, who is with you, O Judah and Jerusalem!' Do not fear or be dismayed; tomorrow go out against them, for the LORD is with you! (2 Chronicles 20:17 New King James Version)

Many times, over the last several years, the Lord has prompted me to see a vision in my spirit. It is basically the same vision every time I see it. It's an army gathered together on a field of review. It's a vivid picture filled with sound and color. I can see the uniforms. I can see the flags that identify each unit. I hear the flags as they flap in the wind. I can see the horses standing at attention, but yet their hoofs ready to move. Everyone is standing at attention and ready to receive their orders. The  vision ends. I know the Lord has been prompting my spirit and preparing my mind to embrace an image that refers to the coming battles that we will fight as his Kingdom Warriors – the Ekklesia[19] – His church. The last time I saw this vision was near the end of August of 2020. The one thing that had dramatically changed in the vision was that the commander in chief had arrived on the field. It was a great lion. He was pacing back and forth in front of the troops. The lion was watching and ready to roar. Interestingly, the Hebrew month beginning at the time of this vision was the month of Elul. It is primarily identified as the time when the King is in the field. I believe the King,

---

[19] The Ekklesia. The purpose of this booklet is to focus on the task the Lord has set before us, especially as the Ekklesia of Texas. The word "ekklesia" is the Greek word which translated to "church" in English. It is a governmental and military term used in the Greek city-states that refers to the calling together of the people for instruction and orders, and then sending them out to transform the culture into the Greek mindset. This is to be the role of the church – the Ekklesia.

our King, the Lion of the Tribe of Judah, is making us ready for the battle ahead. It's time for war. Key passages that the Lord has continually brings to mind are Psalm 110:

> *The LORD said to my Lord,*
> *"Sit at My right hand,*
> *Till I make Your enemies Your footstool."*
> *The LORD shall send the rod of Your strength out of Zion.*
> *Rule in the midst of Your enemies!*
> *Your people shall be volunteers*
> *In the day of Your power;*
> *In the beauties of holiness, from the womb of the morning,*
> *You have the dew of Your youth.*
> *The LORD has sworn*
> *And will not relent,*
> *"You are a priest forever*
> *According to the order of Melchizedek."*
> *The Lord is at Your right hand;*
> *He shall execute kings in the day of His wrath.*
> *He shall judge among the nations,*
> *He shall fill the places with dead bodies,*
> *He shall execute the heads of many countries.*
> *He shall drink of the brook by the wayside;*
> *Therefore He shall lift up the head.*[20]

And from Psalm 149, especially verses 5-9.

> *Let the saints be joyful in glory;*
> *Let them sing aloud on their beds.*
> *Let the high praises of God be in their mouth,*
> *And a two-edged sword in their hand,*
> *To execute vengeance on the nations,*
> *And punishments on the peoples;*
> *To bind their kings with chains,*
> *And their nobles with fetters of iron;*
> *To execute on them the written judgment—*
> *This honor have all His saints.*[21]

On January 2, 2015, I first preached on the word that was eventually given to us as a congregation for the next three years - 2 Chronicles 20:1-17. I preached it again on January 5 of 2018. At that time, we had entered the Hebrew year 5778 (the door or portal) which is the

---

[20] Psalm 110. Scripture taken from the New King James Version®. Copyright © 1982 by Thomas Nelson. Used by permission. All rights reserved.
[21] Psalm 149:5-9 Scripture taken from the New King James Version®. Copyright © 1982 by Thomas Nelson. Used by permission. All rights reserved.

door into the manifestation of the Kingdom. Interestingly, James Nesbit, an artist, created a picture of that door and it was identical to the vision I saw at 33,000 feet in 2016, which I referenced in Chapter One. As I am writing this; we are in year 5780 – Pei (the mouth of the Lord). We will soon cross the threshold of the New Hebrew Year of 5781 (2021).

As I have preached on this passage, the Lord revealed four clear commands that were laid out for Jehoshaphat and the nation of Judah. They are recorded in verse 17.

> *"You will not need to fight in this battle. Position yourselves, stand still and see the salvation of the Lord, who is with you, O Judah and Jerusalem! Do not fear or be dismayed; tomorrow go out against them, for the Lord is with you."*[22]

Stand and Watch – God gives four clear commands!

Station yourselves/Hold Your position (the Hebrew word is yatsav). It means to place, to set, to stand, to set or station oneself, to present oneself, to take one's stand, or to stand with someone. It's the picture of an army at the ready. They have heard the sound of the bugle and have gathered before their commander.

Stand firm (the Hebrew word is amad). It means to stand, to remain, to endure, to take one's stand, to stand still, to stop moving or doing, to cease, to tarry, to delay, to remain, to continue, to abide, to endure, to persist, to be steadfast, and to be appointed. The commander has given the order: "Attention." No moving. No distractions. Nothing but eyes straight ahead and ears ready to hear the orders for the day.

See the salvation (the Hebrew word is yeshua). It means salvation, deliverance, and victory – Jesus! Set your eyes on your salvation. Set your eyes on Jesus. He is the Lord of Angel Armies. He is the King of kings. He is the Commander in Chief.

Do not fear or be dismayed (the Hebrew words are yare and kathath). They mean terror, fear, to be shattered, to be dismayed, to be broken, to be abolished, or to be afraid. Cast off fear. You are endued with the power, presence and glory of God. The battle is His. You will go down to face the enemy, but you will behold the victory of the Lord.

---

[22] 2 Chronicles 20:17 Scripture taken from the New King James Version®. Copyright © 1982 by Thomas Nelson. Used by permission. All rights reserved.

These are the orders given to us as priests and kings, as sons and daughters of the King, our Commander in Chief. We must position ourselves, stand at attention, focus on Jesus and cast-off fear and dismay. We will move ahead as He instructs us – as He reveals His plans through revelation, dream, vision and prophetic insight. As we arrived in the year 5780, the year of the mouth and the year of declaring God's purposes, our focus was now on 2 Chronicles 20:20.

"So they rose early in the morning and went out into the Wilderness of Tekoa; and as they went out, Jehoshaphat stood and said, 'Hear me, O Judah and you inhabitants of Jerusalem: Believe in the LORD your God, and you shall be established; believe His prophets, and you shall prosper.'"[23]

Listen to the prophets and prosper. The portals have opened. We await His instructions.
We see His salvation! We move when He instructs us. We move ahead as the army of God in Texas towards victory.

Move when He moves!

At the beginning of September 2020, the Lord had me focus on two passages from Numbers 9 and 10. The first from Numbers 9:15-23:

> *Now on the day that the tabernacle was erected the cloud covered the tabernacle, the tent of the testimony, and in the evening, it was like the appearance of fire over the tabernacle, until morning. So, it was continuously; the cloud would cover it by day, and the appearance of fire by night. Whenever the cloud was lifted from over the tent, afterward the sons of Israel would then set out; and in the place where the cloud settled down, there the sons of Israel would camp. At the command of the LORD the sons of Israel would set out, and at the command of the LORD they would camp; as long as the cloud settled over the tabernacle, they remained camped. Even when the cloud lingered over the tabernacle for many days, the sons of Israel would keep the LORD's charge and not set out. If sometimes the cloud remained a few days over the tabernacle, according to the command of the LORD they remained camped. Then according to the command of the LORD they set out. If sometimes the cloud remained from evening until morning, when the cloud was lifted in the morning, they*

---

would move out; or if it remained in the daytime and at night, whenever the cloud was lifted, they would set out. Whether it was two days or a month or a year that the cloud lingered over the tabernacle, staying above it, the sons of Israel remained camped and did not set out; but when it was lifted, they did set out. At the command of the LORD they camped, and at the command of the LORD they set out; they kept the LORD's charge, according to the command of the LORD through Moses.

The second was from Numbers 10:35:

Then it came about when the ark set out that Moses said,

> *"Rise up, O LORD! And let Your enemies be scattered and let those who hate You flee before You."*

Once again it is clear that we are dictated by God, our Commander in Chief, to move when He moves. I finished writing this portion of the chapter during the Feast of Tabernacles in 2020 or in the new Hebrew year of 5781. It is extremely important that we find ourselves surrounded by Him in His Tabernacle and listening carefully to His instructions so that we can move out in victory. Rise up, O Lord, and let your enemies be scattered!

5

A Garden and A Gate

Then Jesus came with them to a place called Gethsemane, and said to the disciples, "Sit here while I go and pray over there." And He took with Him Peter and the two sons of Zebedee, and He began to be sorrowful and deeply distressed. Then He said to them, "My soul is exceedingly sorrowful, even to death. Stay here and watch with Me."
(Matthew 26:36-38 New King James Version)

And I also say to you that you are Peter, and on this rock I will build My church, and the gates of Hades shall not prevail against it. And I will give you the keys of the kingdom of heaven, and whatever you bind on earth will be bound in heaven,
and whatever you loose on earth will be loosed in heaven."
(Matthew 16:18-19 New King James Version)

Before we proceed with God's plan for Texas, I need to share an essential defining point in my understanding of prayer that took place while I was ministering as pastor at Grace Lutheran Church in Abilene, Texas and at my present congregation, Prince of Peace House of Prayer in Arlington, Texas.
Anyone who has had an experience of prayer over the last thirty years, at some point, must acknowledge the influence of the book entitled <u>Could You Not Tarry One Hour?</u> by Larry Lea.

The exercise of prayer is an exercise in stretching. It stretches your faith. It stretches your vision. It stretches your endurance. Amazingly, most people do not fully understand or enjoy the power and depth of prayer. Knowing the necessity and value of prayer isn't necessarily enough to make it a pleasant or sought-after task. The same was true for me. My prayer life was developing. I was experiencing a whole new realm of worship. But prayer was a hard task. I was used to reading prayers or listening to others read theirs. Praying spontaneously or praying for longer periods of time was out of my comfort zone. If someone had asked me to pray for an hour, I probably would have given them a strange look. Anything but short prayers, mostly read, was uncommon for me. That changed when I read Larry's book. But I did not just read it; I devoured it. I ordered the VHS series (that just dated me) to show small groups at the church. I preached it. I taught it. But most importantly I practiced it. Using the Lord's Prayer as a model, prayer was easily extended to an hour. Prayer and worship. Worship and prayer. The uncommon and essential nature and practice of prayer was becoming more common.

Listen and let God. The most uncommon nature of prayer for most of us is the process of letting God determine the direction of those prayers. All too often we try to set the terms, the topics and the results of our prayers. We will pray "our" lists. We will declare "our" wants. We will determine the answers "we" want. Now please, do not misunderstand me, the Lord hears every prayer offered in any circumstance and from every person, but at some point, He will begin to line up our thoughts with His, our desires with His, our plans with His, our destinies with the one He determined for us before we were born. Listen and let God.

I can remember one instance in my prayer life where I had a list of about four things that I was constantly praying regarding my life, my ministry and my family. I was getting very frustrated because I really wasn't seeing a response from God regarding some of these prayers. It seemed that they were empty and powerless. Why wasn't God answering my prayers? I've already made it known on several occasions that I would have "spiritual temper tantrums" and this was another one which was brought about by this powerless experience of prayer. After fussing and complaining, the Lord simply spoke to me and revealed a very significant truth. He simply said, "your number one on your list is number four on mine." I had to do some serious searching to find out what was on God's list that He wanted me to pray.

In the mid-90s I took up the call to fast for forty days that Bill Bright had called us to embrace. I fasted for the forty days and all I felt that I experienced was a new brand of hunger. But that is not the complete story. At the end of that fast I had a simple idea enter my heart. Let's spend time with the Lord. Profound, isn't it? No programmed prayer events. No pre-determined results. Let us just meet with Him. We started a night watch which happened every Friday from nine o'clock in the evening and ended twelve hours later on Saturday morning. We set no goals except to meet and watch. Sometimes we would have several people gathered throughout the night and sometimes we sat alone. We usually had a constant playing of worship over the sound system, but we did not try to form a worship team or specific prayer leaders, even though most nights were regularly monitored by our elders. But most nights you would see those elders on the pews or the floor reading the Scriptures or quietly watching throughout the night.

Something very uncommon invaded the life of our church. A desire for His presence filled the atmosphere. Our journals were filled with revelations. The Lord began to direct our prayers away from "I want" to "His will." Sometimes we would spontaneously break into worship or praise, and sometimes we were simply overwhelmed by His love. In the midst of it all, He was keeping His word to us. We were beginning to experience His kingdom and His will manifesting in us and through us to the community, state and nation.

Then on one particular night my whole concept of prayer changed. I was reading the story of Jesus regarding the night he prayed in the garden of Gethsemane. I read this story many, many times. The story is at the very heart of Larry Lea's message in his book. I was by myself at around 2 o'clock in the morning, and I had just finished reading the story again when the Lord spoke to me quietly and told me that he wanted me to understand this story. I made the crucial mistake of telling him that I knew all about it. I had preached it. I had taught it. I had mentored it and practiced it. As far as I was concerned there was nothing new to see in it. Wrong answer! He firmly told me to read it again and I did. Then He told me to read it again and again and again.

> *Then Jesus came with them to a place called Gethsemane, and said to the disciples, "Sit here while I go and pray over there." And He took with Him Peter and the two sons of Zebedee, and He began to be sorrowful and deeply distressed. Then He said to them, "My soul is exceedingly sorrowful, even to death. Stay here and watch with Me."*
> *He went a little farther and fell on His face, and prayed, saying, "O My Father, if it is possible, let this cup pass from Me; nevertheless, not as I will, but as You will."*
> *Then He came to the disciples and found them sleeping, and said to Peter, "What! Could you not watch with Me one hour? Watch and pray, lest you enter into temptation. The spirit indeed is willing, but the flesh is weak."*
> *Again, a second time, He went away and prayed, saying, "O My Father, if this cup cannot pass away from Me unless I drink it, Your will be done." And He came and found them asleep again, for their eyes were heavy.*
> *So, He left them, went away again, and prayed the third time, saying the same words. Then He came to His disciples and said to them, "Are you still sleeping and resting? Behold, the hour is at hand, and the Son of Man is being betrayed into the hands of sinners. Rise let us be going. See, My betrayer is at hand." (Matthew 26:36-46 New King James Version)*

As the story unfolds, Jesus enters the garden with the eleven disciples. He gives a simple command to them to simply sit while he goes further into the garden to pray. The command is simple. In the Greek the word "sit" means "to sit." He then took Peter, James and John further into the garden. The command He gives to them is also simple. He invited them "stay here and watch with me." The word for watch in the Greek is *grēgoreō* and it simply means "to watch" or "to give strict attention to." When Jesus returns to them, he asked them, "Could you not watch with me one hour?" The key revelation the Lord was showing me that night after reading and meditating on this passage for over an hour was simple – He was not asking them to pray for an hour. Whoa! He had asked them to watch Him pray. After that revelation, He then informs them that now it's time to watch and pray so that they would not enter into temptation.

The effect of this revelation on my personal prayer life, the prayer life of my congregation and the prayer life of the network was profound. As I further studied the gospels, I noticed one simple fact. Many times, the Lord had gone off to pray, but He had always done it alone. This was the one time that He had invited three of His disciples to come into that personal place where He would be talking one to one with His father. He literally wanted them to watch and listen to Him pray. And they fell asleep. I personally have no proof of the other revelation, but I believe that one of the disciples, possibly the youngest, had been able to stay awake longer. I believe that John the Beloved was able to hear Jesus pray the prayer that is recorded in John chapter 17 - **the high priestly prayer**. The Lord is inviting us to watch and listen to him interceding for us before the father.

What a novel idea! As we are seeking direction for our personal lives, for our business, for the members of our family, or for the direction of our state and nation, how profound it would be if we would first ask the Lord, "What are you praying, Lord? What is on your heart? What are your strategies? What is my destiny or the destiny of my state or nation?"

At The Gates

We need to know "the destiny" because the Lord has posted us, as gatekeepers, at the gates of our home or business or state or nation. And the only way we can learn the destiny is by hosting His presence or watching Him pray or spending those times in His throne room. I deal with a fuller understanding of gatekeepers and gates in my book, <u>Keeper of the Keys</u>,[24] but let me share some important insights and

---

[24] You can order this book through Amazon. It comes in paperback and Kindle.

reminders.

I've spent many an hour with Jesus at Caesarea Philippi. Caesarea Philippi, located in the northern portion of Israel, is the location where Jesus met with His disciples and asked them, "who do people say that I am?" It was there that He declared to them how He would build the Ekklesia and how the gates of hell would not prevail against what He was building.

Those hours I spent (and still spend) with Jesus were divided into times when I physically was at the location, and other times, when I would meet with Jesus one on one in His presence. In instructing people on how to listen to the Lord or how to spend time in His presence, I've encouraged them to remember a place that they had personally visited and inviting Jesus to meet with them there. Many times, in my living room, I have sat there by the head waters of the Jordan River, at the foot of Mount Carmel, and Jesus and I have had long conversations. It's in those times that He has shared with me many strategies, revelations and understandings.

It is there at the physical location of Caesarea Philippi where you will find what is called the "gate of hell." It's a large cavernous area that once held the Temple of Pan. It is possible that Jesus, as He was instructing His disciples about the Ekklesia, that He actually waved with His hand and pointed at that very gate of hell. It was in that place that He began to reveal to me how important it is that we take possession of the gates on behalf of God's Kingdom. If you don't possess the gate, you cannot witness the fullness of His destiny for that place – your own life, your home, your business, your state or your nation.

Two other locations in Israel where the Lord very clearly defined for me the meaning of the gate is at Megiddo and Dan. In both of these areas, that have been archaeologically uncovered, you can witness the true significance of the gate. Many times, when we think of the word 'gate', we think of a single door-like structure that opens up into your front yard or into a field, but the gate of a city was a large structure that guarded the entrance into that city. You can witness this structure firsthand at both Megiddo and Dan. Picture yourself walking up to the wall of a city and going through the outer doors. As you go through those doors you will enter into a large room or a large area much like a small atrium. Around the walls of this room is a stone bench and on the other side of the room is another doorway that actually enters into the city itself. In that room, in ancient times, you will discover the elders of the city.

They would be sitting on those benches and they would be discussing and carrying out the business of the city.[25] They would be talking about the strategies of the city. But they would also be watching carefully to see who was going in and who was going out of the city. It was their job to make sure that what came in or what exited the city was good.

And in the same way, we are to guard, both physically and spiritually, the gates that God has entrusted to each one of us. As a husband and father, I have been entrusted with the responsibility of guarding the gate of my home and the lives of my wife, my children and my grandchildren. As business leaders, we have been entrusted to guard the gates of our business both spiritually and physically. And as apostolic leaders of a state, we have been entrusted to guard the gates of our state both physically and spiritually. I shared with you earlier that as my wife and I traveled around the circumference of the state of Texas, there were many places where the Lord had us stop and to prayerfully take authority over that entry point into the state.

Over 20 years ago I started meeting with four or five other pastors and leaders[26] in the city of Arlington and Tarrant County. Every Tuesday we gathered together for fellowship, for prayer and for a meal. We developed a strong relationship with each other as covenant brothers. But about six years ago, the Lord revealed something to us that took us to another level as a gathering. He told us that we were not just to meet for prayer, fellowship, laughter and a meal, but we were to see ourselves as elders of the gate of the city of Arlington and Tarrant County. We were to listen carefully to Him, and prayerfully consider what we needed to release into the atmosphere of the city that would ensure that the gates of the city were secure. We took our responsibility seriously and made sure that the gates of the city we're open to Him and that anything that was contrary to Him would need to leave.

It has been amazing to witness the transformation of the spiritual atmosphere of this city and county as we have faithfully prayed as keepers of the gate – elders at the gate. All of our leaders over city government, our Chamber of Commerce, our school district and over all emergency services are dedicated Christians. Our city leaders, on several occasions, have publicly declared Jesus to be the Lord over Arlington. Our work is far from done, but we will continue to take

---

[25] Boaz would carry out business on behalf of Ruth at the gate of Bethlehem in Ruth 4:1. "Now Boaz went up to the gate and sat down there; and behold, the close relative of whom Boaz had spoken came by. So Boaz said, 'Come aside, friend, sit down here.' So he came aside and sat down." (New King James Version

[26] I cannot express with words the covenantal love I share with Jon Bunn, Burton Purvis, Hollis Kirkpatrick, Sam Dewald, Chris Shields and Jorge Lorenzana. Others have joined us from time to time, but these have remained steadfast.

seriously our role as elders at the gate. It is the same role that I take seriously as the director for the Texas Apostolic Prayer Network.

On October 28, 2020, Hollis Kirkpatrick, one of the Elders at the Gate sent this dream:

> All of us were sitting around the "elders table" at Prince of Peace House of Prayer. We were discussing all the keys Tom has in the office and the reality that Schlueter means "keeper of the keys." In a silent moment before us on the table appeared a brilliant cross. It was physically about 12" tall. The cross section was about 8" across. The shaft portion was about 1" square. When the Cross appeared we heard Father say, "The only Key I've given that each of you need is The Cross!" Father had me take the base of The Cross and individually plunge the top portion into the chest of everyone around the table. Each time it was plunged into the chest cavity the brilliance of The Cross never diminished! Once everyone had received the Key of the Cross, the dream ended.
>
> I had forgotten about the dream until Burton Purvis called and stated that he thought God had given me a "key" to a prophetic word that had been given to him...I submit that we are all in a movement of The Cross being the only Key we need to walk in His identity.

Let me summarize this chapter by once again recalling the opening revelation. The only way that we can be a successful elder at the gate is by knowing Jesus intimately and spending time with Him. We are to watch Him as He prays over that assignment to which we have been entrusted. Watch Him. Listen to Him. Decree what He has decreed.

6

Wielding the Axe

If the axe is dull,
And one does not sharpen the edge,
Then he must use more strength;
But wisdom brings success.
(Ecclesiastes 10:10 New King James Version)

We now move deliberately into Texas' story. Let me state again that this will not be a total spiritual history of Texas. We know that the founders of this state, even though entwined in false masonic structures, saw that God had a special destiny for this state. As it developed first as a nation – the Republic of Texas – and eventually as the twenty-eighth state of the Union, it has kept its course in alignment with God. Texas, even as the United States, has made it share of mistakes, but God has in store for us a destination for the manifestation of His kingdom. The same is true for your state of residence.

My part in this story actually starts four years before the network formed. In December of 2003, Dutch Sheets and Chuck Pierce were in San Antonio, Texas. They were carrying out the assignment that the Lord had given them to release the prophetic destiny of the 50 states of our nation. During that meeting, Dutch spoke the following prophetic word:

> "Jesus, we want more of Your Christ anointing of the prophetic. Jesus, the Prophet, come to Texas. Come with Your holy zeal, come with Your fire, come with Your revelation— Jesus, the Prophet, the Prophet of God. The very testimony of You is the Spirit of prophecy. Jesus, come and mantle Texas tonight with another level, another degree of the prophetic anointing to be forerunners for America. Impregnate this state with a transformation anointing. Impregnate this state with the ability to prophesy and decree change to the rest of the nation. Impregnate this state with revelation so that their words don't fall to the ground. Impregnate them with a power that no

matter what the hordes of hell say, that something changes in the Spirit. The decrees of man, the unrighteous spirit, the decrees of ungodly judges begin to pale and fall before You. Let the idols of man fall and be broken next to the Ark of Your Presence. Lord, I just say according to Your word, a nation could be born from this state. I say there is a governmental anointing on the state of Texas—on the Church of Texas—to rise up in her position in heavenly places and begin to legislate and begin to affect, to begin to release the government of God (that) changes the government of man."[27]

As mentioned in the introduction, Apostle and Prophet Chuck Pierce asked me to oversee the prayer network for the state of Texas, and in June of 2007, in the auditorium of our state capital in Austin, Texas, he commissioned me for my new position. As the network began, we emphasized the gathering together and the networking of intercessors from across the state. This had never been done at this level. Even though there were many intercessors praying throughout the state, there had never been a specific gathering or networking of them. We now have over ninety coordinators that oversee sixteen regions in the state. We have a rough estimate of nearly 30,000 intercessors that are covenantally connected via email, social media and most importantly, face to face. The Lord began to develop our vision.

The Texas Apostolic Prayer Network desires the people, the history, the culture, and the destiny of the State of Texas to be transformed as the Lord is enthroned in our midst.

Over the first several years of the network the Lord sent us out on specific assignments to secure the boundary, the rivers, the gates, the counties and other designated locations that needed to be visited, prayed over and brought into alignment with the Lord's Kingdom. I'll be listing some of those assignments here simply to show you the scope of what we faced those first few years. Again, I share them not as a formula, and not as something that each state must also do, but to give an indicator of how important it was for us to listen to Him as he started aligning Texas.

I already shared with you that during the summer of 2007, my wife and I traveled the 3200 plus miles around the boundary of the state of Texas. He asked us to secure all the gates of the state which included highways, rivers and other entry points that needed to be secured. That same year, Chuck Pierce presented to me 254 metal stakes or vavs

---

[27] Releasing The Prophetic Destiny Of A Nation: Discovering How Your Future Can Be Greater Than Your Past by Dutch Sheets, Chuck Pierce, Destiny Image. Page 47

that he declared needed to be planted into the ground of each of the 254 counties of the state. As our leadership council started taking formation in late 2007, the Lord told us to go to the four gates, North, South, East and West, of the state and open them to the King of Glory. In 2008 we joined in alignment with the other 49 states of the nation in going to each masonic Lodge in the state and divorcing that structure from what God was intending to do in Texas. We used a divorce decree that had been written by Jerry Mash and Apostle John Benefiel out of Oklahoma and the Heartland Apostolic Prayer Network. Also, during that year, we began the process of going to all of the heads and mouths of the major rivers in the state of Texas, asking the Lord to cleanse them from all impurities. We claimed Interstate 35 that goes from Laredo all the way up to Minnesota as a Highway of Holiness (Isaiah 35). We carried a branding iron of glory, via worship and prayer, to all of the 16 regions of the network.

In the following years we secured the El Camino Real de Los Tejas, the King's highway that went from Mexico City, through the heart of Texas, and into Louisiana. We took a large team representing intercessors from Mississippi, Louisiana and Texas to re-covenant our states with Israel. The Lord started connecting us in very deliberate and specific ways with legislators, the Attorney General, the Lieutenant Governor and the Governor of the state of Texas. One of our state representatives in Austin secured a room in the State Capital for us to regularly pray into our government and into the legislative workings of our senators and representatives. We have traveled the border of Texas and Mexico along the Rio Grande River. We have gone to each one of the 254 courthouses of the state and made sure that each of them was lined up with the foundations of God's throne - righteousness and justice.

Many other assignments have been carried out across the state and into the surrounding states and into the nation by teams of our network. There are too many to list. The Lord was and is releasing the kings and priests of the state to manifest His kingdom in Texas and beyond. The Lord is creating in us that which He prophetically decreed years ago through Apostle Dutch Sheets and Apostle and Prophet Chuck Pierce during that fifty-state tour. Other words they prophesied, while in Texas, are the following:

> *"There is a mantle on Texas to bring forth change in America. I say there is a governmental anointing on the State of Texas – on the church of Texas – to rise up in her position in heavenly places and begin to legislate and begin to affect, to release the government of God that changes the government of man."*
> *(Dutch Sheets)*

"There is a nation in your loins, and you will birth a nation. God is giving you the authority to address giants who are stopping it. There will be a grassroots movement from Texas that will be seen throughout the nation and the Giant will be addressed. It will be known that from Texas a nation was birthed, a nation went to war, and a nation had the victory." (Chuck Pierce)

We must be directed by the will and the word of the Lord. The Lord is the one who directs us. The Lord is the one who reveals his heart and His strategies to us. As we draw close to Him as priests, He will release our strategies as kings. Prophetic revelation and decree have directed our steps in Texas. Therefore, it should be obvious, that the most essential strategy that we carry out as apostolic prophetic intercessors, not only in Texas, but across the nation, is hearing and obeying the word of the Lord. He and only He is the one that can prepare us. I referred earlier to the difference between the dropping of bombs in World War Two and the laser directed missiles of today. The Lord is the one who can sharpen those tools. He is the one, through the sword of His word, who can cut through the darkness, the confusion, the structures and strategies of the enemy.

On Sunday morning, January 5, 2020, in the midst of my morning devotions and sermon preparation, the Lord started showing me a picture of a sword that have been brought out of its sheath and was being polished and sharpened. As I was meditating on that picture, the Lord showed me an arrow, a flint pointed arrow, that was being chiseled and sharpened. I barely had finished seeing it when He showed me a round being chambered into a rifle. He then declared, "I have sharpened the sword of my people. I have sharpened the tip of their arrows and I have chambered a round into their rifles. Now is the time for the sword, the arrow and the rifle to be used. This is my word which I created for my people to decree and to speak out with my authority."

Later that same month he released a word to our network through Apostle Clay Nash that we were like an axe being sharpened. I will share more on this in a moment but let me say now that during the summer of 2020 the Lord spoke to me a very clear word: "the axe is sharpened." The vision has been set. The Lord reminded me of the time when we were on Comanche Peak in Granbury, Texas, August 8, 2008, and how a Comanche by the name of Shade Large performed a rifle dance which reset vision over the state of Texas. The rifle signified the going forth of God's word and setting forth His kingdom in Texas and beyond. Comanche Peak is a significant location for Native

Americans since it was a location where they would seek direction for their tribes. That was twelve years ago. It's time for the apostolic and prophetic authority to be fully released into and from the state of Texas. The Lord has made it clear that the sword is sharpened, the axe is sharpened, and it's time for war.

The Lord spoke to me and declared, "The tide has turned. I've brought you, Texas, to the turning point. Now is the time to birth the nation in your loins. Rise up Texas into your destiny." He started revealing to me the turning points of our history as a nation. The Lord had already spoken through me that "Texas is the fulcrum point for the nation. That we will rule in the midst of our enemies." That quote refers to Psalm 110:2 which I referenced earlier. The fulcrum is a point of balance or a turning point. It is like a hinge. Here are some of those turning points or fulcrum points for our nation.

It starts with Cape Henry, Virginia where in 1607, Rev. Robert Hunt planted a cross on the shore and declared: "We do hereby Dedicate this Land, and ourselves, to reach the People within these shores with the Gospel of Jesus Christ, and to raise up Godly generations after us, and with these generations take the Kingdom of God to all the earth. May this Covenant of Dedication remain to all generations, as long as this earth remains, and may this Land, along with England, be Evangelist to the World. May all who see this Cross, remember what we have done here, and may those who come here to inhabit join is in this Covenant…"

We can point to Valley Forge in 1778, the Alamo and San Jacinto in 1836, Little Round Top at Gettysburg in 1863, the Battle of Midway in 1942, and D-Day at Normandy in 1944. These are just a few of the extremely important turning points in the history of our Nation and State. There are also those turning points that are specifically spiritual in nature as they established the early covenant roots that the Lord was placing down into our nation that was to produce fruit pleasing to the Lord and His Kingdom. One of those was Cape Henry. We can add to that list locations like Plymouth, Philadelphia, Saint Augustine and Boston

We are standing now at another fulcrum point or turning point for Texas and the nation. Now is the time to go to war. A few years ago, I was touring the Pacific War Museum at the Nimitz Hotel in Fredericksburg, Texas. It is one of the most comprehensive presentations of the Pacific war I have ever seen. One of our greatest Admirals, Chester Nimitz, was born there in Fredericksburg and was the key to the victory "turning point" at Midway. As I came around one of the displays, the words almost flashed off of the wall – TEXAS GOES TO

WAR!

I referred to this earlier, but in January of 2020, Clay Nash shared a dream where I, Tom Schlueter, was standing and working at a grindstone. He said, "I could not see what was in front of him, but I could see the sparks flying. He noticed I was there, and there were sparks just flying everywhere and when he turned around, he had an axe-head in his hand that he was sharpening. And it wasn't just an axe-head like I've ever seen, it was the state of Texas. And out of Arkansas and Louisiana I saw a hickory handle attached to it. Tom was putting an edge to this axe-head. When he finished, he turned to me and he said, 'I want you to finish it with the wet stone, because you use a wet stone that uses oil.' He said, 'Because you have the oil to bring that fine edge that's needed for what's ahead.' So, I believe Tom represents the apostolic, and, I believe, the fine edge is the prophetic, and I don't believe it was me, it was the prophetic that's going to put that fine edge on it, you know, it's very important."

Interestingly, not long after that, as I was spending time with the Lord, the Lord revealed to me **that the sharpening of the axe had been completed**. We were no longer dealing with something that was going to happen in the future but was turning right now. And the axe was as sharp as the edge of a surgeon's scalpel.

Over the next few chapters I will share and give comment regarding certain prophetic words that have been spoken to and through Texas that I believe are significant for this turning point season. I wholeheartedly believe in the nature of the prophetic that even though it may have been spoken to a specific person, church, state or even nation, it has the ability to penetrate into the heart of any that hear the word. As you hear these words, I pray that you will pray that they will be fulfilled in our state, but you will also embrace them for your state and for your ministry as well.

Atmospheric Domination and Apostolic Displacement Authority

Hannah Sheets, Dutch's daughter, in August of 2019 decreed over Texas, "We have atmospheric domination. We aren't just called to come into a 'place.' We are called to rule there. It's time to get in over your head. Get to the higher place and rule from there, not to there."

> Dutch then said, "We must be a company that fights well. There is a mantle on Texas to bring change to America, to legislate and anoint. The greatest year of war will be 2020. It will be vile. Our response level needs to be just as powerful

or more so than the enemy. We need to decree eternity and keep decreeing. This is a warning for the nation. 2020 will be one continual siege that will release what God is going to do. May the ancient markers of our founders be restored. We are a covenant nation. Therefore, the next move of God will be more than getting people "saved." It will be about recapturing a nation. There were places where covenant was established in the land. Places that are markers of God's purpose. Texas needs to visit these places of covenant...calling forth those roots!"

One of our coordinators, Jimmy Dusek, had released a couple of years before that the Lord was giving us apostolic displacement authority. In other words, wherever we journey, with His Spirit and with His authority, He displaces the darkness, the death and the strategies of the enemy with His authority, His presence, His glory and His life.

Hawks and Eagles

Another prophetic picture of this time of turning or shifting took place at my home in Arlington, Texas. Our church and home property in Arlington have been guarded by hawks. They allowed me to get within 10-15 feet of them. I would walk from my home to the church next door, these hawks would follow me and nest on the roof or in the trees outside my office. In prophetic symbolism, the hawk represents victory, freedom, a warring attitude, a keen and discerning spirit (hawk eye), acute awareness. The hawks, as they matured, extended their territory. The Lord has spoken clearly to me that it is time for the hawks and eagles to soar.

During the second weekend of September 2020 I joined leaders down on the southern border of Texas along the Rio Grande River. A word had been given to Esther Gallegos of Laredo that we needed to release the Eagles from Eagle Pass, Texas. As we released the eagles, the Lord began to speak clearly that he was causing His church, the Ekklesia, to leave their roost and their nest and to soar into the heavens. There he would give us clear eyesight and precision warfare to see what needed to be declared into the world below us. We are seated with Him in the heavenly places. We are soaring with him in the heights. He doesn't bring us up high as an escape mechanism from the darkness that we are living in. He causes us to come up high with the wind of the Holy Spirit under our wings in order for us to see the darkness and decree the word of the Lord and his light back into that darkness so that it will be dispelled and dismantled and that God's Kingdom and his awakening will be released in the state and in the nation.

Dutch released this word from his brother Tim Sheets, over us as a Texas leadership council in 2018.

> "An incredible force is being released on the earth by our great God. There has never been a warrior force like it in history. God says they are going to be called my "War Eagles ". They will make up My eagle force, and that eagle force will partner with my Angel force and my remnant warrior champions. There is coming now a generation of young warriors that will partner with the remnant warriors who have been championing the call for years. They will ride the waves of My glory. They will ride the currents of My winds...the out-rayings of My presence, and they will begin to manifest the works of My Kingdom. They will demonstrate My power: they will accomplish My will, My way, and they will ride My tsunami wave ablaze with My glory. Not one kingdom will be able to withstand them. My unique eagle force will startle the world with the intensity in which they stand for Me. The coming generation of "War Eagles" have been groomed and reserved for hell's siege on earth; and they will now be loosed. They will not bow to the enemies of their God. They will not pay tribute to enemy kings. They will not listen to the propaganda and insults of hell, and they will not allow Me to be lumped in with other gods which are not gods."

The Sound of Reveille

This war season was highlighted even more at a leadership advance in August 2020 for our TXAPN council. Becca Greenwood released words over our council that carried us into the heat of the battle. The best way to summarize it is to write out a transcription of an assignment that was carried out after that retreat at the East Gate of our state near Tyler, Texas. We gathered at a boundary marker that was placed in that location in the mid 1800s and is an actual international boundary marker between the old Republic of Texas and the United States of America. It also was an international boundary between Spain and France. It represents the East Gate from the state of Texas that goes into the heart of the nation and to Washington D.C. This is a portion of the transcription from the vision that Becca saw and the comments of others as we carried out this assignment.

Becca Greenwood wrote:

> "I saw Jesus standing above the South. I heard the Lord say, 'To establish the South, and particularly to Texas, you are a gateway of this nation and what is established in the South will reverberate across the nation all the way to Washington, D.C.

It is a season of being re-established as a righteous gateway for the nation. Where it has been an entry point for evil along the border, this evil is being shut off. I then saw that the sex trafficking at the border will be dealt with. The entity of Santa Muerte (god of death) that has tried to come into our nation through the borders of Texas, that door of evil will be shut! He is awakening the gateway authority of the South, a spiritual position of standing at the gate. In the days ahead, it will no longer be a gateway of contention, but a gatekeeping authority will continue to rise up within the church, within the prophetic, and within the intercessory army. What is unfolding within the government of Texas will have an effect and impact all the way to the Nation's Capital in D.C."

Becca then declared,

"I'm going to start with that sound piece because those of you that were at Tom's event. I'm not going to do tons of teaching today but reverberate actually comes from two Latin words... *'verbe'* and *'rare'* and it means a sound. The original means, 'a sound and a rod of authority.' So, what comes forth from what we reverberate is a sound that is literally a rod of authority that pushes back, casts back or lashes out. So, we push back the darkness and allow God's Kingdom light to come in. It shifted in later days into just being a sound word. So, everything that is coming forth today, we decree right now, that we are reverberating out from this governmental foundational stone of this region, we are reverberating out across the nation that it is a new day of a new sound of a covenant of the gateway authority of Texas that will rise up governmentally in the natural, that is rising up governmentally in the Ekklesia with the apostolic prophetic, that we are here today to set into alignment what you have called for this new era from the gateway of the South.

Tom Schlueter said,

"Back in January, Clay Nash had a dream that included me where I was.... he saw me fashioning something in a blacksmith shop and it was an axe head in the shape of Texas. Then he saw a hickory handle coming from Louisiana and Arkansas and attaching to it. We are planning some kind of a gathering in March where the three states will come together to do this. Well, we've been praying into that word that the axe was going to cut whatever needed to be cut in this season. Then three weeks ago, Cindy Jacobs, not knowing that word, gave a word that Texas is the axe head and we will be on the front lines what happens not only here but into D.C. and will release much like a Cane Ridge revival throughout this whole area.[28] And the axe has been very important to us and the Lord said that the finishing has been done on the axe. It is now ready to cut." Well, yesterday when we were with Gary and RaJean Vawter and Kerry and Diane Kirkwood at the Reformation House of Prayer in Tyler, Ed Morris, who plays the trumpet for them at that meeting, played Reveille. Becca said, "Oh, are you kidding me?! You can't make this stuff up!!" Then Ed said, "In the musical field, the trumpet is called the axe."

Becca went on to say,

"So that transpired at the TXAPN meeting, so you know what we're doing with sound right now as we were going this direction. We were driving from the airport to the meeting and we flew into San Antonio and I heard a sound....it was late, Greg and I were traveling late....and I heard Reveille playing out in the atmosphere and I said, "Greg, what is that bugle song, that military bugle call, because I didn't know. That song, you know that song "da ta da da," do you know it? He said, "Reveille!". What is so amazing is that Reveille is also a French word that ties into the sound of the word reverberate. And it literally is, "wake up!", and we didn't know that it was the sound of the axe and all of this prophetic tying in together. So, Tom, decree into that.

I decreed,

"Father, we apply your axe. You decreed to us there in Fredericksburg, Lord, that your apostolic prophetic troop, the watchman warriors in this hour are the axe! It is not a physical axe, it is the axe of the apostolic prophetic movement, the government of God that is now set on its perfect edge and is cutting through the darkness! It is cutting through the entanglements, it is like a scalpel going into the body and making sure the heart is restored from its trauma and distress and we release that today here, Lord, that sound. Let it

---

[28] And here is the word Cindy Jacobs spoke: "The Lord would say, 'Texas, you are My battle axe. You are My shield. I am pouring out My Spirit upon you to protect the nation. I am pouring out the spirit of a warrior upon TXAPN. Gird your loins, be strong, because I have you on the forefront; you are frontline. I am not having you at the back of the battle, you are on the front of the battle. Your prayers are availing much. This state will be on fire for the gospel. I am getting ready to light gospel fires that are going to spring up in so many little places.

reverberate, let it be like Reveille that sounds from this place and restores the nation, brings it back into Kingdom alignment, brings it back into true governmental alignment in the Name of our King and our Lord Jesus Christ."

It is time for Apostolic domination and authority. The axe has been sharpened. The trumpet has sounded. It's time to go to war. In the following chapters, we will examine other prophetic words.

52

7

Cutting With His Words

Where there is no revelation, the people cast off restraint;
But happy is he who keeps the law.
(Proverbs 29:18 New King James Version)

The Lord promised, as we entered into the year 5778 (2018), that we would have a fresh and powerful outpouring of prophetic revelation like never before in and through the State of Texas. This has been especially true for Texas, as a Prophet State. There have been many words, visions and dreams of the words of the Lord going like lightning bolts into the rest of the nation. People have heard bells, tuning forks, new sounds and vibrations shaking the heavens and the earth. All across the state we have heard  testimony of signs, wonders, miracles, transformations that are being birthed. We are witnessing a new era. We've never been this way before. The turnaround is happening. God's kingdom and will are being manifested on earth as in heaven.

Every year at our retreat (advance) I present a video review of what the Lord released to us the previous year and what we can expect to come in the future. As I was planning the video summary for that year, I was hoping to reference many of those words, but the number and length of the words made the task seem impossible. So, throughout the video I provided short phrases and declarations that summarized a longer word. The important issue for us, as a state, is that we obediently decree and legislate those words that the Lord has given us. Two keys words from the Scriptures that the Lord has highlighted to me in the last few weeks are Job 22:28 and Psalm 149:5-9.

And in this chapter, I am only including a few of those words from the last four years – 2017 to the present.

PEY (PEI)

We dealt with the gates of Texas in 2008, but sensed this was a new era, twelve years later. Twelve is a governmental, apostolic number.

We had to make sure that we have the gates opened in this Pey (Pei)[29] Era to the right things and closed to the wrong things. We opened the gates at Texarkana, El Paso, Laredo and Amarillo. The crown has been placed on the state - there is no King but Jesus. Shake the nation, Lord, with this prophetic declaration.

At the beginning of the Hebrew year of 5780, Nate Johnson of Australia declared, "The other night as I was worshipping, I saw a very clear vision of a map of the state of Texas, and the Lord was allowing a magnifying glass to hover over it. I felt instantly that He was brooding over it because it was birthing something significant and mighty—something He had always seen that this state would bring forth. What I was drawn to, right away, was God's magnifying glass. It was enlarging and magnifying what He was doing, causing the world to look and see something that shouldn't be hidden. It was too precious to Him, and He wanted it seen. It has always been said that "everything is bigger in Texas," yet what God is doing there is even beyond what we can comprehend. There is a move of the Spirit that is going to erupt in Texas, and it will be a sign and a wonder to the world."

The Lord desires the Ekklesia in all of the states of this nation, not just Texas, to be a force for his Kingdom. Each state has a gifting and destiny that God designed in each state at the beginning which needs to be utilized in the bringing forth of His kingdom and His will on earth, as it is in heaven. It is essential that each state discover that identity and that vision and carry it out so that God can move through our nation with his love, compassion, grace, glory, power and transformation.

Over the rest of this chapter, and the following chapters, I will focus on some of the revelations, prophecies and strategies and the Lord has given to us. This again is not meant to be a formula but simply a testimony what the Lord has done with us and what he will also do with you in your sphere of influence. Note that in some cases I give further explanation and context, but in other cases I simply share the word followed by the one who gave it.

Tribunals

The Lord is developing and transforming TXAPN from solely a prayer network into a movement. He then revealed that we were to be a

---

[29] The Hebrew number for 80 in the Hebrew year of 5780 (2020) is the seventeenth letter Pey of the Hebrew alphabet. The Word Pey means "mouth" used in word, expression, vocalization, speech, and breath". This has several significant prophetic emphases for year 5780 as it signifies that prophetic revelation and the declarations of the Lord will be especially important to heed.

collection of tribunals, that legislate from kingdom authority into the regions, the state, the nation and into D.C. There's that word tribunal. The definition of tribunal, many times used in the military, is a Court of Justice. As we've carried out intercessory assignments across the state, the Lord declared to us that He was establishing legislative councils across the state. He then gave us the word, tribunal. These tribunals are taking the shape of representatives coming from several counties around the state into one location, and in that place, legislative decrees of justice, righteousness, strength, truth and the Kingdom decrees of the Lord are released. The synchronization and synergy of those gatherings have literally "shaken our meetings," and we are beginning to see things shake in the natural such as the changing of leaders in government, the shifting of weather patterns, the release of key strategies for cities and even our nation.

Hurricanes Ike, Harvey and Laura

in September of 2008 we were attending the last three days of a 90-day period that had been set apart by Dutch Sheets and his congregation in Colorado Springs to be exclusively a time of worship and prayer for the nation. During those days, I received word that a powerful hurricane was heading towards Galveston. It was hurricane Ike. As I always do, I asked the Lord what prayers or declarations needed to be made regarding this storm, and his answer was, "Look at the name." I was not quite sure what He meant, but I started researching the name Ike and the first thing that came to my mind was General Eisenhower, who went by the nickname of Ike. I was still not sure what this meant, but in looking up the name Eisenhower, it refers to one who works with iron or stone. The Lord then revealed, "I am circumcising the nation as a covenantal act." It was interesting that the storm was going to hit Galveston and the port of Houston which is a part of the birthplace region of the TXAPN. Even though we always pray for God's divine protection through these powerful storms that hit our coast, I knew it was important at that moment for the sake of our state and our nation to invite the Lord to circumcise us.

In August of 2017 a category four storm named Harvey made its way towards the Texas coast. Once again, the Lord had us look at its name and the place of its arrival on the coast. Consider that the name Harvey means "battle ready." The Hurricane hit land between Rockport (Jesus is the Rock) and Corpus Christi (the Body of Christ) to show the world and His Body that He is the Lord and there is no one like Him. Prophet Lana Vawser of Australia sent me a word at the time of the storm. She wrote:

"The tide is turning in Texas. I am coming in a way I have never come in before. I am coming in a way you have never seen before. ... I am going to make a way where there is no way. The tide is turning in Texas. The ground the enemy has occupied in Texas is being uprooted." I am releasing the manifestation of the new day of destiny written in the scrolls of Heaven over you, Texas. As this storm has come to devastate, I am coming to ACTIVATE—to activate a greater tipping point of breakthrough upon you, Texas. The TRAIN OF MY ROBE will FILL TEXAS.

The idol of religion is coming down. I am striking down the spirit of religion, and where it had its greatest hold, I am raising up FOUNTAINS OF LIFE and My living water, and many will come to DRINK of My salvation and revelation—from ALL over the world."

And finally, in August of 2020, Hurricane Laura came on land in Louisiana just East of the border with Texas. This was an interesting storm structure. There were actually two hurricanes moving through the Gulf of Mexico at the same time. One was called Marco and the other, Laura. Laura should have arrived first, but Marco passed her by. Marco means "war" and it was headed towards the coast. But as it arrived, it miraculously dissipated into nothing. Laura which means "victory" followed soon after. It eventually became a category four hurricane and while praying, the Lord revealed to me a picture of the storm and its path into the nation. It looked like a giant shofar or trumpet that was about to come into the land. It would go up between Texas and Louisiana, and then head east over Tennessee and Kentucky and significant revival centers of the past including the Cane Ridge meeting house. It would end up in Washington D.C. Reveille is sounding. The trumpet is blasting the sound of victory from the birthplace regions of our nation on the Gulf Coast into the heart of the nation and onto its capital.

The Tuning Fork and the New Sound

I had mentioned in a footnote earlier that my last name, Schlueter, means "keeper of the keys of the prison." Many times, on different assignments the Lord has had me carry a key, buy a key or use a key for the unlocking or the locking that needs to take place at that location. I very rarely go anywhere without a key. In 2018 the Lord sent me on assignment to Cape Henry on the Virginia coast. I was looking through my keys to see which one I needed to take, and the Lord said: "I have given you a new key for this season. It is a sound key. It will pierce the atmosphere and the land, and it will cause doors that have been shut like iron to break open."

He then told me to find a tuning fork I had purchased years earlier. The tuning fork key of 444.4 Hz is often called "the Key of David." It is a double portion of Isaiah 22:22.[30] It was sounded there at Cape Henry, the U.S. Capital, the Texas State Capital, Point Loma in San Diego, the covenant well at Beersheba and at the East (Sheep) Gate of Jerusalem. The Lord declared: "I, the Lord, have assigned the anointed priesthood after the order of Melchizedek to reestablish My covenant with this state and nation." The tuning fork is normally used to bring instruments, especially pianos, into the right frequency. Proper alignment is a must and the sound of the tuning fork was bringing that alignment.

And, with perfect timing, Lana Vawser of Australia wrote: "There is a NEW SOUND arising out of Texas. The Lord showed me that this new sound that is arising out of Texas was the sound of worship to the King of Glory. It was the sound of worship that had not been heard before. It was such a deep, weighty, sound, a sound of worship that carried a breaker anointing… and there was a cry coming out of the hearts of thousands of believers that was deeper than they had experienced before."

Pharaoh, Baal, Jezebel and Abortion

The Lord through his prophetic revelations to us has given us the ability to dismantle strong powers and principalities of darkness. I share next an experience that I had in the state capital of Texas when the Lord literally took me into a third heaven location. In the Spring of 2016, we were praying our normal prayers of blessing and wisdom over the leaders of our state and nation. In the midst of our prayers I was lifted up above the gathering of intercessors and I was told in no uncertain terms that we were not to pray "that way" over those leaders.

The Lord revealed to me the "Pharaoh" spirit or structure behind the governmental leadership of our state and nation. He commanded us to go to a new level of apostolic and authoritative prayer to dismantle this structure. As we did, other next several months, we witnessed the shifting of our national government via President Trump and the eventual announcement of resignation by two key leaders of the Texas House. But God made it clear that we are a significant part of the ongoing dismantling of a false structure in our nation.

Weeks later I had the following dream:

---

[30] *The key of the house of David. I will lay on his shoulder; so, he shall open, and no one shall shut; and he shall shut, and no one shall open. (Isaiah 22:22 The New King James Version)*

"I saw an old structure that needed to be demolished and everyone was excited. A wrecking ball started doing its work and the walls began to crumble. I saw inside the building and there was an older woman sitting on a chair. There was a sensing that everything needed to stop so that she would not be harmed. As I set my gaze on her she looked up and I saw her eyes glaze with red, and I knew that we were dealing with an evil structure. The more I concentrated on her, the more I heard comments that the wrecking ball should be stopped for fear that we might harm this woman. The chair she was sitting on was like a throne. At first, I did not see what seemed to be an invisible structure around her that kept her protected. As the image ended, I sensed in my spirit that everyone believed that the wrecking ball must stop."

After the dream, I started reading my assigned daily Bible readings. It was from Isaiah 13 about the destruction of Babylon and Matthew 24:15-31 about the "abomination of desolation." The Lord reminded me of a vision I had two years ago of the new armor He was placing on us that was diamond like and brilliant with light for taking down darkness. I shared the dream with Dutch Sheets and Chuck Pierce. In response, Dutch commented: "I have been thinking about this, Tom. I agree with you. This woman is the Jezebel/Baal structure over our government that has protected the evil structure that rules. May it be demolished! No fear of shutdown." And Chuck declared: "Let the ball begin!"

Merrie Cardin of Brazos Covenant Ministries in Granbury, Texas and a lead apostolic leader of TXAPN had an open vision. She writes:

"I heard: 'Texas, our Texas, all hail your mighty King' (in the literal tune of the Texas State Song – 'Texas, Our Texas'). Texas will contend with the beasts of Ephesus as Paul did and be triumphant. I then saw a large rodeo arena. I heard the announcer and knew it was Jesus. He called loudly for all participants to come to the arena. Some people came down from the stands and Jesus was pleased because the season to be a spectator for pleasure was over. This arena was the church. There was a cry for intercession that arose for the pouring of new wine, and then more and more came from the seats into the arena. Then the lights in the seating area went dim and became dark. Some were still there, but they were now in the dark. This was grievous to me. But there will be some who will not heed the call to leave the seated places and engage the new wine war. The audience must be transformed into the activity of Jesus arena. Now it became very solemn, and as I looked, the bull pens opened. This was not to be the entertainment of bull riding but the arena of wrestling the bulls. This scene reminded me of a rodeo I saw at the Comanche Nation. There was an activity where there were three circles and men of courage stood in those circles. Bulls were loosed and the last man standing won the prize. In this vision the bulls were turned out and we turned to do face to face confrontation with what I knew was Baal. 'Texas, do not fear to go face to face and contend with the Baal systems on behalf of the nation. Seek My face and do not fear their faces. I will allow you to be up close and personal in this war, but I will give you the victory.' I saw that we were triumphant, and we walked away with the horns as spoil of war. Somehow, they became our next weapons. I know that will become clearer."

Along the same theme, Ruby Dodson, one of our coordinators from Corpus Christi shared the following:

"I see a stump of a tree that has been chopped off at about three feet. The stump is in the Dallas area. It is dirty and moldy looking with no live shoots. The tree, when it was healthy, had roots going in all directions. When a tree gets chopped down, it sends its life out to the roots and new trees sprout up all around it. I believe the Lord is revealing "the tree is the shedding of innocent blood, the abortion tree". We are dealing hard blows to abortion.

On June 24, 2018, the Lord sent a team of seven of us to the old Federal courthouse in Dallas. This was the courthouse that was used to send the decision of Roe v. Wade onto the Supreme Court. We decreed as kings and judges – appointed by God – to overturn the ruling of Pharaoh. We decreed his demise just as the first Pharaoh was destroyed. And we asked for a witness of the act. We decreed (1) that rain would fall, (2) that life would be promoted and (3) that within days a change would take place on the Supreme Court. IT DID ALL THREE! The next day, with zero percent chance of rain, it rained. The next day in a miraculous decision out of California a decision for life was made. Soon thereafter Supreme Court Justice Kennedy left the court. The next week in a vision, I saw the Lord remove the LIFE tape[31] from Matt Lockett's mouth as they stood in silence before the Supreme Court. The Lord placed it on the month of the opposition. "I will silence them with LIFE and open up the mouths of the saints to decree

---

[31] Matt Lockett and his teams from the Justice House of Prayer in Washington, D.C. stand at attention on the sidewalk in front of the Supreme Court. They are silently declaring the end of abortion.

the presence of God's kingdom."

The Turnaround, Awakened into the New Season

Over the last several years, there has been a very predominant and strong message to the church that it's time to turn around. It's time to awaken. It's time to enter into the new era of glory that has been destined for you. These words have been spoken over the nation and even the nations of the earth, but they were also spoken very directly to the church in Texas. Following are prophetic words, revelations, dreams and exhortations that were given to and from Texas.

> "The church has functioned far below her destiny, but this is about to change! The spirit of wisdom and revelation is increasing in the church and will bring full realization of our position and purpose. I believe this Turnaround gathering is a First Fruits of this; we will hear the will and instructions of the Head, and as His governmental voice, decree it for Him into the earth. One prophecy concerning the upcoming Turnaround conference stated that the worldwide prayer movement will be launched into its next phase. Functioning as Christ's Ekklesia IS that new phase! The Church is about to move into a completely new level of enforcing kingdom rule and the will of God on earth." (Dutch Sheets)

"We decree the turnaround. I decree the downfall of Soros and any other provisional stronghold that is supporting evil in this land." (Tom Schlueter)

"The wells of the past will spring forth with new life. Watch where religion has covered up the movement of the Spirit. These wells will spring forth!" (Chuck Pierce)

Dallas has long been known as a place of death because of the Roe v. Wade case and the assassination of President Kennedy, but Bill Johnson of Bethel Church in California decreed: "Dallas, you have been called by God as a miracle center. You have been called by God as a city that burns with revival. This revival is not just in one place or just a big church but churches all over the place...I feel like you (Dallas area) are going to have a unique gift for mental illness to be healed – in this area."

> "The Lord declares that if Texas will let me deal with their two major sins - pride and independence - I will use this state to change the nation. As Texas has repented of pride and independence, the Lord declares that a seed has indeed been

planted into the ground and died. It will now spring forth as a righteous tree that will manifest God's kingdom to the nation." (Tom Schlueter – June 2018).

"Out of Texas, I will send forth My Winds. I will sweep this Nation in a Wave of Glory that the like of has never been seen.   Bend your knee to Me, Texas. I want to use that fierce, bold spirit of yours for My Purposes.   Leave behind your man-made agendas and embrace the Higher Call.   You are a Firebrand in My Hand, Texas, one that I will use to set this Nation on Fire for My Glory. My LOVE will sweep this land breaking down every high place and demolishing strongholds and every thought which seeks to exalt itself against Me. You are a spearpoint, Texas. One that I will send into the heart of darkness in a Flame of LOVE so powerful, so encompassing, the darkness cannot comprehend it ... nor overcome. You are a LOVE LETTER I have set in motion, the voice of the Prophet crying out in the wilderness calling a Nation back to her covenant root with Me. I honor you, Texas, because you have stood with My Firstborn, Israel, when others have not.   You have remembered My Promise to Abraham of old. Bend your knee to Me, Texas, and Kiss the Son. As you surrender all that you are to My Holy Fire, as you allow My Spirit to purify you to the core, out of the flames you shall arise: STRONG, TRUE, FURIOUS LOVE, MY FIREBRAND OF GLORY!" (Intercessors at the Heart of Texas House of Prayer)

"I saw the fire of God branding believers and the words burning in the fire of God were the words "FIRST LOVE". As believers were being branded by the fire of God, and idols, captivity, lies and chains were breaking off believers with significant increase, I noticed the angel of awakening was standing in their midst. All hands-on deck. This move of His Spirit was moving so powerfully drawing the body of Christ from all different areas, denominations and streams together in one accord, deeper unity all for the extension of His Kingdom and His Glory seen. A multigenerational, multifaceted move of the Spirit of God. He is relentlessly pursuing His people, awakening them, awakening the cry for more, and releasing beautiful outpouring. Such a beautiful purification, purging, impartation and commissioning was taking place in the lives of God's people. Suddenly I had a vision and I saw again thousands upon thousands upon thousands of believers all across Texas raising their voices releasing worship to the King... It was the sound of VICTORY! It was a war song that was ushering in a MAJOR move of the Spirit of God throughout Texas bringing forth mass deliverance, healing and freedom." (Lana Vawser)

"God has re-established His heart in Texas. Seeds have been planted and watered and are coming into fruition. And yes, while there is still resistance, we know how the story ends. The atmosphere has shifted, and the enemy wars now in desperation. His gates won't hold against the people of God who know and stand in their identity in Christ and exude His Love." (Kim Ulmer, Heart of Texas)

Words of Precision

On our morning TXAPN prayer call, the Lord was speaking to us regarding precision. He is bringing precision to the Ekklesia. While at Texas A&M University, I remember watching intently as the National Champion Fish Drill Team went through their precision drills. When the Ekklesia moves in precision, the world will be attracted to us. The precision of the Ekklesia depends on our obedient faith relationship with our King - moving with precision at His revelatory orders! (Tom Schlueter)

You are NOW contending from this place, rather than contending for it. I am holding you as a scepter in my hand. My authority will be released through this state. (Tom Schlueter – Fall 2018)

On September 16, 2020, Clay Nash saw a vision. He wrote,

> "Tom, I awoke this morning seeing 254 on the ceiling. I was not aware of its significance until I researched. I discovered Texas has 254 counties. This I did not know. I searched Strong's number 254. This is what God is saying, based on the definition that that word ("halusis" in Greek and "ach" in Hebrew), God is saying that Texas is becoming His firepot to break the chains that bind the hands of Godly authority in the Nation."

I saw the Lord holding playing cards. In His hand were all the highest trump cards. The enemy was rejoicing in their victories as they played the smaller value trump cards. But the Lord laughed and declared: "I hold the final trump cards." (Tom Schlueter)

The enemy tried to bury us, but he was not aware that we are a seed of God. (Tom Schlueter)

Find your voice. Better yet. Find your SHOUT, a make a difference. (Dutch Sheets)

Awakening is coming. It is ready to be released. Prophesy hovering life. Activate the anointing and birth the future. Plow with the ripper or deep plow. There is a holy ripper plowing through hard pan. We have everything we need to finish the job - to turn this nation. America shall be saved! (Dutch Sheets)

Today I'm resetting this nation to move into the position that I have long desired to see them in. For in the past there have been efforts on my behalf to position that which I've called for, what I have called the land to birth, but those efforts have fallen short. But as I reset this nation today and I humble this nation and bring them to their knees, I have positioned this nation closer to my heart. From this day you will walk in a new level of authority. You will walk in a new place. You will walk in humility and love beyond anything you have ever known in the past. (Ken Bryan)

The Tide Has Turned. The Lord has dismantled and dislodged the serpent at top of the Texas triangle. The Lord is sending arrows to critical locations of our state and nation. (Tom Schlueter)

The new era is here. Moses is dead. You've never been this way before. You are standing before the Commander of the Angel Armies. Get behind Him – not in His way. (Tom Schlueter)

Border

Earlier I shared how the Lord established a new gate at an international boundary in the northeast section of Texas where France and Spain, the Republic of Texas and the United States was once marked. Borders are especially important in the new era. The Lord Himself has declared that He has determined our boundaries.

> *"And He has made from one blood every nation of men to dwell on all the face of the earth, and has determined their preappointed times and the boundaries of their dwellings, so that they should seek the Lord, in the hope that they might grope for Him and find Him, though He is not far from each one of us; for in Him we live and move and have our being, as also some of your own poets have said, 'For we are also His offspring.'"*[32]

---

[32] Acts 17:26-28 New King James Version®. Copyright © 1982 by Thomas Nelson. Used by permission. All rights reserved.

Boundaries and borders are both physical and spiritual in nature. I recall to your memory that the first assignment the Lord gave us was to drive and secure the border of Texas. He had previously given me a similar assignment of driving and walking the border of the City of Arlington. He sets out our spheres of influence. We are to secure the boundary and the gates that enter in and exit those boundaries. In Biblical times, the Lord appointed the elders of city to carry out this task. For the last twenty years, He has assigned a group of us (apostles, pastors and ministry leaders) as "Elders at the Gate." We take seriously what the Lord is revealing good or bad that desires to enter or exit the sphere of our influence.

Chuck Pierce declared:

> "What the real war is over right now is advancing the Kingdom. The border wars ahead are intense. Then the Lord said 'watch Texas' because of the border. Texas was our only sovereign type nation that we have in this nation. There is some sort of rule and authority that Texas has to set as a prototype for the entire nation. Now I'm telling you it's going to happen at the border, I can prophesy that to you right now. It's going to happen along the border and what you see happen in Texas will be a precedence from state to state and the states that reject it, they are going to be in big trouble."

Several of us have driven the southern boundary of Texas and even joined teams driving the entire southern border of our nation. Once while we stood by the Rio Grande River, the Lord declared through me: "From the river is coming life, redemption, justice, courage, and salvation. It is not a dividing line between nations but like a major artery in the body that is pumping life to the entire body! We pull life out of this river - overturning the Pharaoh spirit. The political and religious - bound together in this place - has been dismantled! A historic shift has taken place at this vav point along the river!"

A New Authority

The Lord has given us new authority as apostolic and prophetic watchmen. One of those days when we were gathered in the State Capital, I was summoned to the office of one of our state senators. I was gifted with a replica chair from the Constitutional Convention of Texas in 1876. It was presented to me by Texas Senator Brian Birdwell[33] in March of 2019. He declared over Tom, "This chair

---

[33] Senator Brian Birdwell is serving as a Texas State Senator but is a Lieutenant Colonel in the United States Army. He was badly burned during the 9/11 attack on the Pentagon.

represents the new authority being given to you for Texas and beyond."

In a dream, I was standing in the courts of Heaven. I had been unsure of an assignment that the Lord had given me. I was certain I was not smart enough for the very technical task before me. In the dream, the Lord spoke me (and to all of us):

> "Tom, I've given you a scroll of strategy. You have fears and thoughts in you that you are not 'smart enough' to attend certain meetings. You're right. You're not, but I've given you something better – My presence and My wisdom. I will place you in strategic meetings and places as I always have but now, I'm taking you to a higher level of authority. You're not just opening doors but bringing My presence and wisdom through those doors. Trust Me! Be seated in My presence, Tom. Enter My Courts with confident joy. I will unseal the scroll at its proper time. But I have given it to you. Dutch will help unlock it. It is meant to unlock the true prophetic destiny of Texas." Interestingly, after that dream, He has taken me into locations previously "locked" to my entry.

And through Chuck Pierce, He laid out an important aspect of our assignment: "Now I'm going to go ahead and announce this, 'over the next two years we are going to see a lot of governmental upheaval. It's going to make us see how powerful the Lord is. Don't try to go in and straighten out the enemy, people, that's going to get you in big messes. I see God's people trying to get all the enemies of this nation straightened out – let them turn on themselves. Let them take each other out. I'm telling you God is saying this to us.'"

> "I then heard the Lord ROAR loudly again and this time as He roared, I heard the declaration being made in the Spirit: 'ALL DELAYS BROKEN! ALL DELAYS BROKEN, NOW I DECREE ACCELERATE!' Many have heard My ROAR. Many have heard the RHYTHM of My ROAR and are interceding what My heart is decreeing, and it is CHANGING a NATION from the inside out, it is changing the nation from the inside out. This new day of commissioning upon the United States is about to burst forth and in this new commissioning I saw a MIGHTY DECREE being stamped upon the nation. 'UNITED STATES OF AMERICA! THE NATION THAT CARRIES THE JUSTICE OF THE LORD.'" (Lana Vawser)

"The Lord is lancing the boil and the evil is being exposed and removed. Do not fear the foul evil. God is cleansing. He is bringing forth His kingdom." (Tom Schlueter)

"The dividing sword of the Lord has been unleashed." (Robin Durham, TXAPN Coordinator from the Heart of Texas Region).

> "I Am putting in My people the ability to put out hell. Even though hell is raging, and fire is rising from the earth, I Am giving My people a sound and a movement that will cause hell to recede. I will have a people who know how to communicate through the airways. I will have a people who know how to rise and decree that I will triumph! You're still flying too low and I must have a people who come up to a place to hear the songs that have never been heard. So, rise up! For as you blow up the enemy's plan, you will hear the sound of victory that will enter the earth. I Am creating a new communication network throughout the earth. Position yourself on the communication line for I have lines around the earth that I Am speaking from heaven." (Chuck Pierce)

"Lord, You have been speaking through your prophets that "the fullness of the Amorites has come," and the penalty for these practices, of incest, sexual immorality, adultery, idolatry, blasphemy, homosexuality and bestiality, is death. We yield to Your leadership, Lord. The Lord will go forth like a warrior. He will arouse His zeal like a man of war. He will utter a shout, yes, He will raise a war cry. He will prevail against His enemies." (Darla Ryden, Coordinator from TXAPN Birthplace Region))

> "We have been given a Divine commission and authority – a spirit of power and might, like Jehu who was a man of spiritual ranking and authority. I felt we, TXAPN – tribunal, were to SMITE the house of Ahab. Let me remind us here: We cannot overcome something in the land without first taking our own "land". We must overcome this structure in ourselves first, so be prepared to see some things in yourself. I saw us as a group rising up in a Jehu anointing. 2 Kings 9:20 tells us that Jehu had a "SHIGGAON" tenacity.   He went furiously after his target and even drove his chariot like a madman.   There was no compromise and no turning back. Jehu would not quit until he dealt with the entire house of Ahab and Jezebel." (Ginny Bryan, TXAPN Lead Apostolic Team Member))

"I heard the Lord say, 'I am releasing scrolls of revelation and strategy right now that will set up My people for the next ten years! Pay attention! In this encounter I kept seeing foundations.' The Lord then spoke, 'The foundations that I lay through the revelation contained within these scrolls for 2020 are the foundations for the decade so they must be implemented correctly." The commissioning of the eagles will take place from the upper room. These eagles will be sent forth to uncover and reveal My truth.'" (Lana Vawser)

> "I Am sending My angels, and they are preparing the ground for breakthrough. They are opening up the wells that I have placed in your region that have been capped by the enemy and capped by religious demons. But they are peeling back the layers, and they are opening up those old wells. And those wells will now spring forth, and you will move into the spheres of influence that I have purposed for you." (Tim Sheets)

"The top of Texas, the Crown of Texas, the Panhandle is very central in the United States and this sound, like a fountain was going up and covering and flowing over the entire country. When we make a sound this month of Pey, this decade of Pey from the Panhandle, from the Crown today, I believe that sound is going to reverberate not just through Texas, but, into the nation." (Lonnie Brooks, TXAPN Coordinator from the Northern Panhandle "The Crown")

> The favor and unlimited authority of the King of Kings IS being given to us in a fresh way in this year of 2020 that we might take this enemy plot down. As we act on His wisdom and warning about the vote in 2020, He will show us that this is a new level of maturity and authority being received and released in a way we have never experienced before. (Bob Long, Director of Rally Call Ministries and TXAPN Lead Apostolic Team))

8

Midway and the Alamo

"The great truth that was coming to His servant with ever increasing clearness was that the Holy Spirit can only make intercession through those human temples He indwells; also that He can never intercede in any arbitrary way, but only just as far as His channel can become one with Him in so doing."[34]

Earlier I shared with you that the Lord had called our congregation, and later the network, a "strategic house of prayer." He was establishing us as a place that would strategize and network intercessors together whether that be in the context of a local church, a city or a state. And our ultimate assignment was to be on the frontlines of the Ekklesia as it brings forth the kingdom of God and His will on earth as it is in heaven.

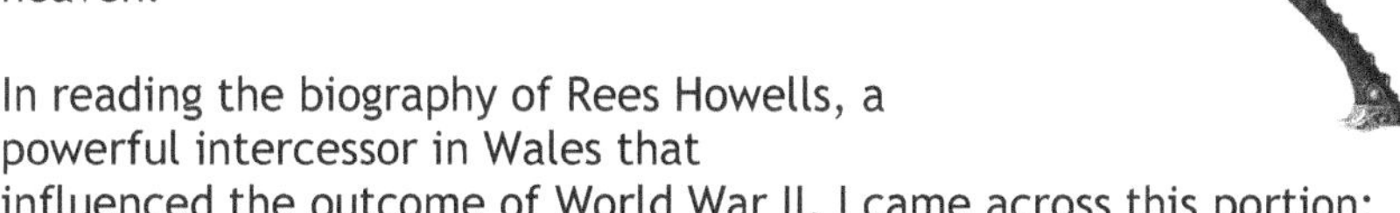

In reading the biography of Rees Howells, a powerful intercessor in Wales that influenced the outcome of World War II, I came across this portion:

"Their prayers became strategic. They must face and fight the Enemy wherever he was opposing freedom to evangelize. God was preparing an instrument—a company to fight world battles on their knees. The first battle of prayer on this international scale was in 1936 when Germany sent her soldiers into the Rhineland and broke the Locarno Treaty. "We knew that France would be on fire in a day," said Mr. Howells, "and it meant nothing less than a European war, and the consequent hindrance to the spread of the gospel. Only those who were in the college can realize the burden the Holy Spirit put on us. 'Prevail against Hitler,' He said to me, and it meant three weeks of prayer and fasting." The daily diary of the college meetings at that time records this prayer battle March 21. Things are very black on the Continent. We pray on until eleven o'clock in the morning, and come back at two thirty in the afternoon, and six and nine o'clock in the evening. We ask the Lord to deal with Germany. March 23. Very grave on Continent and in London. Meetings at nine and eleven o'clock in the

---

[34] Rees Howells, Intercessor by Norman P. Grubb, CLC Publications, Page 91

morning, and six and nine o'clock in the evening. We plead
with God to deal with Hitler and the German nation, and to
bring them to account. March 24. Situation regarding European
crisis very black, all the countries are disagreeing with each
other. Burden is coming on very heavy, but the Lord is allowing
us to plead the Every Creature Vision in His presence. The Lord
turns our eyes off the countries to Himself. Meetings at nine
o'clock in the morning, and six and nine o'clock in the evening.
It continued like that for another five days. Then on March 29,
Mr. Howells came into the meeting and said, "Prayer has
failed. We are on slippery ground. Only intercession will avail.
God is calling for intercessors—men and women who will lay
their lives on the altar to fight the devil, as really as they
would have to fight the enemy on the Western Front.""[35]

On October 8, 2020, my wife Kay and I flew to a meeting in
Middletown, Ohio called RESET 2020. The meeting, hosted by Apostle
Dutch Sheets, was a Holy Convocation where the Ekklesia was called to
pray for our nation. This gathering had large periods of time given to
prayer, prophetic declarations, scriptures, worship, etc., as we heard
from heaven and prayed strategically for our nation and the upcoming
elections. As we were in flight to the convocation, the Lord showed me
a vision.

I was spending time abiding with the Lord in His tabernacle, and He
began to tell me to disrobe. He said to me, "Just as you took off the
robes of Lutheranism, take off every other robe of culture, mindset,
religion, sin, fear, shame and stubbornness. I'm disrobing you so that
you will stand naked before Me in My tabernacle – covered only with My
glory! Once again as you are high above the earth, I am reminding you
of the new diamond like armor I've placed on you. I am resetting you
and My Ekklesia."

I saw earlier that same week the Lord removing the old garments of the
church, even back to those placed on the church by Constantine. It
reminded me of the Lutheran pastor Peter Muhlenberg taking off his
clerical robes. According to a biography written by his great-nephew in
the mid-19th century, on January 21, 1776 in the Lutheran church
in Woodstock, Virginia, Reverend Muhlenberg took his sermon text from
the third chapter Ecclesiastes, which starts with *To everything there is
a season...;*" after reading the eighth verse, "a time of war, and a time
of peace," he declared, "And this is the time of war," removing his
clerical robe to reveal his Colonel's uniform. Outside the church door
the drums began to roll as men turned to kiss their wives and then

---

[35] Rees Howells, Intercessor by Norman P. Grubb, CLC Publications, Pages 262-263

walked down the aisle to enlist, and within half an hour, 162 men were enrolled. The next day he led out 300 men from the county to form the nucleus of the 8th Virginia Regiment.[36]

A **convocation** (from the Latin *convocare* meaning "to call/come together", is a translation of the Greek ἐκκλησία *ekklēsia*) is a group of people formally assembled for a special purpose, mostly ecclesiastical or academic.[37] We gathered there to receive and carry out the orders of the Lord of Hosts. It is time to war if we desire peace. After the meeting in Ohio we once again boarded a flight to go to Washington DC, but we had a layover at midway International Airport in Chicago. As I was walking down the concourse, there was a display about the Battle of Midway and I was immediately drawn to it. As I wrote earlier, it was and is a turning point for the history of our nation. Hanging from the ceiling was a Douglas SBD-6 Dauntless airplane that was used to bomb the four Japanese carriers. The word dauntless means not to be daunted or intimidated, fearless, intrepid and bold. This defines who we are as kings and priests, sons and daughters of the Most High God.

Let's go from Midway to the Alamo. While at the Alamo Mission in San Antonio, Commander William B. Travis issued a letter signed "Victory or Death" and dated February 24, 1836. At the Alamo in San Antonio, then called Bexar, 150 Texas rebels led by William Barret Travis made their stand against Santa Anna's vastly superior Mexican army. On the second day of the siege, February 24, 1836, Travis called for reinforcements with this heroic message. But little help came. Santa Anna's troops broke through on March 6. All of the defenders of the Alamo died. This historic letter was delivered from the Alamo to Texas by Captain Albert Martin of Gonzales.

> *Commandancy of the Alamo*
> *Bejar, Feby. 24th. 1836*
> *To the People of Texas & All Americans in the World—Fellow Citizens & compatriots—*
> *I am besieged, by a thousand or more of the Mexicans under Santa Anna — I have sustained a continual Bombardment & cannonade for 24 hours & have not lost a man — The enemy has demanded a surrender at discretion, otherwise, the garrison are to be put to the sword, if the fort is taken — I have answered the demand with a cannon shot, & our flag still waves proudly from the walls — I shall never surrender or retreat. Then, I call on you in the name of Liberty, of patriotism & everything dear to the American character, to*

---

[36] https://en.wikipedia.org/wiki/Peter_Muhlenberg
[37] https://en.wikipedia.org/wiki/Convocation

come to our aid, with all dispatch — The enemy is receiving reinforcements daily & will no doubt increase to three or four thousand in four or five days. If this call is neglected, I am determined to sustain myself as long as possible & die like a soldier who never forgets what is due to his own honor & that of his country —
Victory or Death.
William Barrett Travis.
Lt. Col. comdt.[38]

The year was 1960 and John Wayne's new movie, "The Alamo", came to the big screen. I was eight years old and I was an avid fan of Davy Crockett. It's somewhat interesting to have him as a fan when I was living in northeast Iowa and had no background or understanding of the history of Texas. But I had fought many a battle, like Davy Crockett, on the steps of the church that my dad pastored in Monticello. Iowa.

As a nine-year-old, my interest in Davy Crockett grew even more as my dad took a pastoral call to a church in Dickinson, Texas. I grew up singing the ballad of Davy Crockett. I had one of the old Alamo sets where I literally recreated the entire Alamo complex. Oops, I still have that old Alamo set. And now I lived in Texas and was thrilled beyond belief the first time I was able to step on that sacred ground in San Antonio.

I can still remember that first Halloween when I was able to dress up as Davy Crockett, with an outfit that my mom had first made for my older brother, that was complete with the coonskin cap, the shirt and a play flintlock rifle. My life was made complete regarding Davy Crockett when my dad, who had collected antique militaria, gave to me a Kentucky flintlock rifle. I believe I have made the point that Davy Crockett was a very important historical character in my life.

On the morning of September 21, 2020, I had a waking dream regarding Davy Crockett. I'm still unaware if I was with him or if I was actually Davy Crockett. In the dream I was with a group that had arrived in the North Texas area from Tennessee. A choice had been placed before us of which direction we would take as we continued to head south. I rose up with confidence, as Davy Crockett, and said "we will proceed to San Antonio. Even if it means our death we will go where the Lord wants us to go." The dream ended. Later that morning in prayer I thought of Esther. "Then Mordecai told them to reply to Esther, "Do not think to yourself that in the king's palace you will escape any more than all the other Jews. For if you keep silent at this time, relief and deliverance

---

[38] https://www.history.com/news/travis-writes-from-the-alamo-victor

will rise for the Jews from another place, but you and your father's house will perish. And who knows whether you have not come to the kingdom for such a time as this?'"
(Esther 4:13-14 English Standard Version)

After reading this dream, Dutch Sheets declared: "We must wear this mantle!"

> Then later that day, I received an email from Andrea and Jim Lafferty and their blog: The Political Sifter. Jim Lafferty wrote: "Some mornings as I say my morning prayers sitting on the side of my bed, I feel like Davy Crockett on the Wall at the Alamo staring out at a vast sea of Mexican uniforms. Washington, even as I write this, is the Alamo 2020 where a handful of brave men and women are standing against a diabolical foe which this country has never seen in our history. (You know you are headed for a complicated day when a sizable number of your opponent's list "Sorcerer" as their occupation). Let me get right to the point. <u>We need reinforcements here on the front lines</u> of the Culture War. Our Lord has introduced me to a whole new group of heroes. They are all Americans and they follow the schematic of great Americans…ordinary people doing extraordinary things with God's direction. My wife and I operate on the principle that with God on our side our Marxist opponents are hopelessly outgunned but, still, it would be good if all those people who encouraged us to undertake this confrontation would show up for the main event. You may get some people now that everyone sees that you're not getting beaten up," one Christian activist counseled us. As you read this, please search your soul and **make plans to come to D.C. soon to help** us confront the darkness of the political souls in this town. And come here, in person, to stand with us and the one leader who is being subjected the full-blown wrath of the Marxists…Donald J. Trump, our President. Pray and make a stand with us in the Name of God."[39]

> The Preamble of the Constitution of the State of Texas reads: "Humbly invoking the blessing of Almighty God, the people of the State of Texas do ordain and establish this Constitution.

> Constitution of the State of Texas."[40]

---

[39] Andrea and Jim Lafferty - The Political Sifter, hotline@politicalsifter.org. September 21, 2020
[40] https://en.wikipedia.org/wiki/Constitution_of_Texas

> In Article I: Bill of Rights, Section 2 it reads: "All political power is inherent in the people and all free governments are founded on their authority and instituted for their benefit. The faith of the people of Texas stands pledged to the preservation of a republican form of government, and, subject to this limitation only, they have at all times the inalienable right to alter, reform, or abolish this government in such a manner as they may think expedient."[41]

Donna Craig, one of our TXAPN coordinators, wrote: "As I was reading this *(the quotes from the Constitution of Texas)*, I felt it was the reason God has said we are to speak prophetically and governmentally into D.C. Our constitution explicitly states the government in our land/state is founded on "our authority" and "we stand pledged to the preservation of a republican form of government"!" It is the reason I heard the "Remember the Alamo" battle cry over our state again. We stand firm as watchmen, laying siege works against the enemy's plans in order to maintain our republican form of government "of the people, by the people, and for the people".

During War Room Prayers[42] on Wednesday morning, August 26, 2020, I was looking up towards heaven and I saw, as though it were, two large hands pulling on an opening in the heavens. I knew that it was the portal that the Lord has established over Prince of Peace House of Prayer. But the hands kept pulling the portal wider and wider. Then I saw the hands opening up other portals around North Texas, and then in other areas of Texas. Finally, it was as though there was a huge portal that God had opened up the size of the state. The Lord is pouring out His strength, glory, anointing, awakening and the mantle for warfare.

On March 6, 2011, I was standing with a prayer team outside the Alamo. The Lord had assigned an initiative where we were to go to all of the battle locations that took place 175 years ago during the Texas revolution. Here at the Alamo we could not go in because of the anniversary ceremonies that were taking place inside, but we circled the old Chapel and decreed what needed to be decreed over this sacred site for all Texans.

I was walking with my good friend Mark Gonzalez who leads a strong and powerful Hispanic prayer network in the nation. As we were

---

[41] Ibid

[42] War Room Prayers are held in my church office every Wednesday as 12-16 prophetic intercessors gather to release God's directives into the city, state and nation.

walking along, we could hear them playing "Amazing Grace" on bagpipes inside the Chapel. The Lord released a word to me. He said, "This battle was not between Texas and Mexico, but was a battle of people gathered together to fight a tyrant - Santa Anna." Mark and I talked about what the Lord had told me as we made our way around the front of the Chapel. At the front entrance the ceremonies were ending and coming out of the Chapel was a contingency of men and women holding up parade banners representing the different states and nations that had been represented there at the battle. At the very front was a man holding a pole and the two banners floating from the top read "Texas and Mexico." We are in that place again where the Lord is gathering together His Ekklesia from all ethnicities to rise up against a tyrant who desires to destroy the church, our state, and the destiny of our nation. Our decree is the same of Colonel Travis - "victory or death."

Reveille has sounded. The portals are open. The axe is sharpened. The oil is ready. The eagles have been released. Texas is going to war. It's time to move. Set your face toward God and get ready to move into the new. Dutch Sheets declared: "We must be a company that fights well. There is a mantle on Texas to bring change to America, to legislate and anoint, to bring all that God's will is in covenant mercy, provision, communication and destiny of being a voice of God. The greatest year of war will be 2020. It will be vile. Our response level needs to be just as powerful or more so than the enemy. We need to decree eternity and keep decreeing. This is a warning for the nation."[43]

The Lord spoke to me throughout the summer of 2020 and declared to me: "In uncertain times, certainty! Expect the unexpected! I've created a movement - you have been launched. You are no longer a network. You are a movement!"

"Texans move to the sound of guns. They are willing to be at the forefront, the tip of the spear when liberty is threatened."[44]

Join the movement! We are wielding the axe and Texas is going to war!

---

[43] A quote from Dutch Sheet's message to the TXAPN Leadership Council in August 2019.
[44] Lt. Col. Allen West, Chairman of the Republican Party Of Texas

9

The Axe is Ready

"And the sons of the prophets said to Elisha, 'See now, the place where we dwell with you is too small for us. Please, let us go to the Jordan, and let every man take a beam from there, and let us make there a place where we may dwell.' So, he answered, 'Go.' Then one said, 'Please consent to go with your servants." And he answered, 'I will go.' So, he went with them. And when they came to the Jordan, they cut down trees. But as one was cutting down a tree, the iron ax head fell into the water; and he cried out and said, "Alas, master! For it was borrowed." So, the man of God said, 'Where did it fall?' And he showed him the place. So, he cut off a stick, and threw it in there; and he made the iron float. Therefore, he said, 'Pick it up for yourself.'
So, he reached out his hand and took it."
2 Kings 6:1-7 New Kings James Version

On October 23-24, 2020 I was attending the birthing of a new tribunal in the TXAPN network. I was in Lubbock, Texas. When I woke up on Saturday morning, the 24th, the Lord was reminding me of the above passage from 2 Kings.

The Lord is revealing that the story is about those that are trying to establish the prophetic ministry – extending it and bringing it into a place of prominence, but they were trying to build a ministry based on their own strength. They are trying to use something borrowed when the Lord  has given each of us this gift. They are trying to expand their ministry when promotion comes only from God. As they are cutting down a tree, the axe they were using breaks and the axe head goes into the Jordan River. The axe head was dull and not sharpened properly.

In January 2017 I preached on this passage and these revelations had been given to me at that time.

We are in season where we are being called into greater effectiveness, greater authority and greater influence. We must prepare for this growth. But we need good tools – a sharp axe. In this story the axe head fell off. It was loose or dull, therefore it was useless and ineffective. Dull axes do not cut well, and they can even bounce back and become dangerous to the user. Abraham Lincoln, known for his skills with log splitting, once declared: "Give me a tree to cut down and six hours, and I will spend the first four hours sharpening my axe." He understood the wisdom I wrote about earlier from Ecclesiastes.

"If the axe is dull, and one does not sharpen the edge, then he must use more strength; but wisdom brings success" (Ecclesiastes 10: 10 New King James Version).

The axe must be sharpened. You must use a sharpening stone or whetstone and either water or oil. The first step in the axe sharpening process is to find the bevel angle on one side of the axe. Then, while matching the bevel angle, start pushing the heavy-duty sharpener against the edge at the proper angle. Make sure to push against the edge and not pull into it, much like when knife sharpening. Apply the oil while sharpening.

The prophetic symbolism here is priceless. The apostolic and prophetic ministry cannot be built by human hands, but by the spirit of prophecy itself. The axe was borrowed. The work was fruitless. The work ended in disaster as the axe head flew into the river - the river of promise and the river that was to be crossed to enter into the promised destiny. BUT, the prophet Elisha calls the axe head out of the water, via a stick, in order that now it can be sharpened and used properly with a new apostolic prophetic edge. It's interesting that word for stick (*ets*) is translated stick, a plank and interestingly "gallows." Is the Lord allowing something to be put to death in order that something new can be brought forth? It's also interesting that the root of this word is *atsah* and means "to shut" like one shutting a door.

We need to witness the sharpening of the axe by the Lord through the apostolic prophetic anointing that only the Lord provides. We cannot build this. The Lord sharpens us by His covenant relationship with us. In Proverbs 27:17, it declares: *"As iron sharpens iron, so a man sharpens the countenance of his friend."* The word countenance here is *paniym* and refers to the "face" of a friend. The Lord, our King, Savior and Friend is the one who sharpens the axe.

Jonathan Cahn, in <u>The Book of Mysteries</u>, helps clarify this process through his devotion "The Secret of the Axe."

> While on one of our walks, we came across a groundskeeper. He was cutting down a small tree with an axe. "'If the axe is dull,'" said the teacher, "'and one does not sharpen its edge, then more strength must be exerted.' It's from the Book of

Ecclesiastes. In other words, if you use an axe with a dull edge, the energy you expend and the power you apply will be spread out, dissipated over a dull edge. The axe becomes inefficient and ineffective. So, to accomplish the same amount of work, you need to spend more time, energy, and force. On the other hand, if the axe's edge is sharp, it will focus and concentrate your power. Therefore, it will take less time, energy, and force to accomplish more." "I'll remember that," I said, "when I cut down my next tree." "You won't cut down trees," he said. "But you'll still need to remember it." "Why?" "Because it can change the way you live." "How?" "Replace the word axe with the words your life. If your life is dull, and you don't sharpen its edge, then more strength must be exerted. A dull edge is one that is less focused. It doesn't converge. And if your life isn't focused, if your life doesn't have a single focus, if it's spread out in many directions or with unclear purpose, then it will have a dull edge. But if you apply to your life the secret of the axe, if you sharpen your life . . ." "How?" "First, you need to have a clear focus and aim. Then you need to bring everything in your life into harmony with that focus and aim, so that everything you do is consistent with that aim and converges to that focus. Then your life will have a sharp edge. Then your life will become powerful. Such were the lives of the giants of Scripture from Elijah to Paul to Messiah. Live life with a sharp axe, a focused edge, and your energy, your strength, and your efforts will be multiplied. Make God the focus and point of everything you do. Make His will the aim of your life, and His purpose the focus of your life. Sharpen the axe . . . and the tree will fall." The Mission: Today, sharpen your axe. Focus your life. Make God and His purposes the point, the aim, and the goal of everything you do."[45]

Jon and Jolene Hamill, in their new book, <u>White House Watchmen</u>, shares how the tenor of our prayers has increased. There is a new urgency of the Ekklesia. The axe is sharpened as we have been awakened in a season of chaos and disorder. They write:

"Throughout the span of the coronavirus pandemic, Americans have been turning to God for support. Praying Psalm 91 and receiving communion have now become national trends. Sunday sojourners are becoming seekers in the secret place. Warriors in the Spirit are sharpening their swords... Even many who never breathed a prayer before are reaching out to God because they want to receive the protection only He can give.

---

[45] The Book of Mysteries by Jonathan Cahn, CharismaHouse, Day 141.

In short, America has awakened in prayer! And we have finally united together to fight an existential threat. President Trump called it a war against an "invisible enemy."[46] I believe this description is more apt than he knows. Within the context of these words, both the destiny of our nation and the lives of our loved ones are at stake.[47]

I hope and pray that you will realize that the axe of your apostolic prophetic intercession is sharpened. I invite you to join the frontlines of this battle.

The Lord said, "I am pouring out My Spirit upon you to protect the nation. I am pouring out the spirit of a warrior upon TXAPN. Gird your loins, be strong, because I have you on the forefront; you are frontline. You are on the battlefront. I am not having you at the back of the battle, you are on the front of the battle. Your prayers are availing much. This state will be on fire for the gospel. I am getting ready to light gospel fires that are going to spring up in so many little places."

---

[46] "Jack Shafer, "Behind Trump's Strange 'Invisible Enemy' Rhetoric," Politico, April 9, 2020, 4: 24 p.m., https:// www.politico.com/ news/ magazine/ 2020/ 04/ 09/ trump-coronavirus-invisible-enemy-177894."

[47] White House Watchmen: New Era Prayer Strategies to Shape the Future of Our Nation by Jon Hamill, Jolene Hamill. Page 20.

10

A Declaration

You will also declare a thing,
And it will be established for you;
So light will shine on your ways.
(Job 22:28 NKJV)

'But the court shall be seated,
And they shall take away his dominion,
To consume and destroy it forever.
Then the kingdom and dominion,
And the greatness of the kingdoms under the whole heaven,
Shall be given to the people, the saints of the Most High.
His kingdom is an everlasting kingdom,
And all dominions shall serve and obey Him.'
(Daniel 7:26-27 NKJV)

During the above-mentioned RESET 2020 in Middletown, Ohio, Apostle Don Lynch of Don Lynch Ministries in Jacksonville, Florida, stood before the gathered Ekklesia and declared the following words. I encourage you to make these declarations from your own heart and mouth on a regular basis. In so doing, you will "Wield the Axe" and release God's purposes on the earth. Many of the following words are specific to the time we are in (October 2020) as we approach the filling of the Supreme Court with a new justice, Judge Amy Coney Barrett, and as we approach the November 2020 election. Decree these words! Add your own as the Lord gives you revelation. Step into the mantle of being a priest and king.

An authentic Ekklesia called into assembly by apostolic order to hear and agree with the announced intentions of the King has come into apostolic order.

Our confession, or mutual agreement is the Apostle and High Priest. We mutually agree that He is both Apostle and High priest.

We do not come now to debate among ourselves. We do not come to an animistic altar hoping to obligate the god of our design to help us.

We come in agreement with the Standing King for the accumulated purposes the prophetic dream pictures as a sealed scroll. We agree that the Word of the Lord for America has been reserved and preserved for this Reset moment.

We agree that Jesus says He is now willing to invest this accumulated inheritance in this generation, in an Authentic Ekklesia, in a New Era Reformation.

We stand in the authority of that agreement with our Apostle, the Architect who carries a full set of blueprints that will produce the original intentions of the Father's eternal purposes.

We agree with the Involved Intercessor, our High Priest, who created all, redeemed all, and now operates in Providence to restore all. We agree with His reset and restoration of Father's original intended purposes for this land.

We come in agreement with the intended purposes of the Inheritor of the Inheritance, Son of God, Worthy Lamb, who rules the nations, the One who formed and founded the United States of America.

We agree with Him that the Creator, not the government, endows us with certain inalienable rights, and agree with Him for the full restoration of these rights.

We agree with Creator Jesus, who invests Father's eternal value in every baby at the moment of conception. Before his momma even knows he is there, Father is there. Father cries, "I want that one!" We agree with God.

We agree that the right to life supersedes any imagined and contrived right to privacy that provides legal justification for the murder, maiming, and marketing of the unborn. We agree that the most dangerous place for a baby in America will no longer be his mother's womb.

We agree that turning has come. The empty seat filled on the Supreme Court will begin a process of reversing precedents, calling every state in the Union to renewed commitment in protecting the unborn from the death row demons who birth live babies to harvest their brains and bodies for money. We agree with Creator Jesus and His planned parenthood.

We agree that the healing of the land has begun. We reject the rejection of children, and this healing will release another post-spiritual-war baby boom and populate our healed and healthy land with hope-filled offspring.

We agree our children and grandchildren will enjoy the fruit of this victory.

We agree with Jesus that media brothel bullies no longer dominate with Leviathan's systematic delusion. That the overkill, unrelenting, sharp Sword of the Lord strikes the seven heads of Leviathan.

We agree that the legal bootleggers who badger us in courts of law will no longer silence our fundamental liberties to preach, sing, worship, and freely express the apostolic Didache of kingdom culture.

We agree that apostolic preaching will announce this Word of the Lord for America, with manifestations of the Spirit's power and impartations of strategic wisdom to mature believers.

We agree that Gospel announcement will pierce the blinding veil over the masses as Awakening rises and hungry people experience a heightened awareness of God, moved by unseen winds of the Spirit, as spiritual arenas over entire regions shift from closed to open.

We agree that this nation is a fathering nation. We agree with God's intentions to restore America as a Remnant nation among the nations, a fathering nation to the nations.

We agree that America is as exceptional as Jesus makes her.

We agree with the dedicatory words of Robert Hunt, that we preach the kingdom Gospel into this land and export the kingdom Gospel from this land.

We agree that America will once again become a premier, missionary-sending nation.

We agree that His original intentions call for the establishing of kingdom culture through which His radical representative Remnant will influence every gate of American culture.

We agree that His Ekklesia and its kingdom leaders in the gates displace the strategically positioned authorities of hell. We usurp the usurpers. We exercise the Ekklesia's establishing authoritative, using kingdom keys.

We also agree that among the several candidates for and men elected to the office of President in our nation's history, few, if any, have agreed with Jesus as much as Donald John Trump. We agree that his agreement with Jesus, as deep and historic as it is, should continue for another four years.

We are ecstatic to agree with both Jesus and our President:

- *We readily agree to bless and stand with our friend and ally Israel;*
- *We stand for the sanctity of life in the womb.*
- *We work to find and release captives of sexual slavery and become a relentless terror to those who enslave them.*
- *We seek significant reforms in our economic and justice systems.*
- *We agree that judges who sit in our courts shall be original-intention Constitutionalists.*
- *We agree that Donald J Trump is the best person to nominate the empty seats on the Supreme Court during the next Presidential term.*
- *We agree that tyrannical Marxist, pirate nations shall not gain power as economic leaders, so they no longer gain leverage to rape the world's economies.*
- *We agree that we will not cower in fear because of a virus being used to terrorize our nation stripping us of the Creator's inalienable rights and calling us to bow down to the satanic religion of evolutionary scientism.*
- *We agree that America's houses of worship cannot be closed by tyrannical state governors and silence preachers and worshipers with political terrorism.*
- *We have not forgotten Dr. King's dream, and we agree with Jesus and our President that racism cannot and will not be the legacy of our generation.*
- *We agree that God sets the borders of nations and the protection of those borders from enemies, without and*

the security of our persons and property within, is the principal reason that We the People made agreements with our government.

- *We agree that any legal definition of "marriage" written without considering the Creator's original design and definition cannot serve as the nation's standard for that covenantal relationship.*

In a vision, I saw Jesus lying down, covered with the dust of centuries that had settled upon Him. I saw Him stand up and shake himself, and the wind blew the dust away, as if it had never been. He set His feet and looked around America with fire in His eyes.

I saw the fire in His eyes. But more importantly, I experienced that fire. It is the burning passion of the Father for this nation. I feel it right now.

"America, God wants you!"

Jesus looked around this land with a challenge on His face and declared to heaven above, earth around, and hell beneath,

"America is mine! America is mine!"

We agree that Jesus involves Himself in history to position a New Era Reformation based upon the apostolic restoration operating at the foundations of His reset, radical, representative Remnant, who decree the Word of the Lord into our nation's spiritual arenas.

The kingdom Ekklesia created a confrontation with the pagan Ekklesia in Ephesus and Asia Minor as Luke records in Acts 19.

Luke summarizes the result: "In this way, The word of the Lord gained momentum through overcoming spiritual might and took dominion.

We agree now that the scroll being unsealed from the Beersheba overflow of Cape Henry will gain momentum through overcoming spiritual might and take dominion in the United States of America!

We agree that a reconstitution of the kingdom Ekklesia restores the intended purpose of Jesus for America. She is a fathering nation and restores America to her place of leadership among other fathering nations.

We agree with Jesus Christ, who says, "I am not finished with America!"

We agree and declare, "America shall be saved!"

If you agree, Ekklesia, shout, "We agree!"[48]

---

[48] Don Lynch, RESET 2020, October 9, 2020 in Middletown, Ohio.

ABOUT THE AUTHOR

Thomas Schlueter has been Pastor of Prince of Peace House of Prayer, a strategic house of prayer in Arlington Texas, for 29 years. Pastor Schlueter obtained a Bachelor's degree at Texas A&M University before receiving his Master of Divinity at Wartburg Theological Seminary. He received his Doctor of Ministry in July 2006 from Christian Leadership University in New York.

Pastor Schlueter's ministry extends beyond Prince of Peace House of Prayer and the Dallas-Fort Worth region. He is the Founder of Arlington Prayer Net, a network of prayer leaders from churches and ministries in Arlington and surrounding communities. The purpose of the network is to come alongside the pastoral staffs of local churches to start, strengthen and expand prayer ministries in the church.

He is the Apostolic Coordinator of the Texas Apostolic Prayer Network (TXAPN), which desires to see the redemptive anointing of the State to flow freely. They desire the people, the history, the culture, and the destiny of Texas to be transformed as the Lord is enthroned in our midst.

He is aligned with Apostle Dutch Sheets and his National Ekklesia International. He serves as the Texas and South-Central United States Regional Leader of the Reformation Prayer Network directed by Apostles Cindy and Mike Jacobs of Generals International. Dr. Schlueter is in covenant relationship with Dr. Chuck Pierce of Global Spheres International. Dr. Pierce set Dr. Schlueter in as coordinator of TXAPN in June of 2007. Pastor Schlueter teaches prayer and Bible seminars locally and internationally.

Pastor Schlueter is actively involved with praying strategically for city government and workplace ministry. He has a passion to see the whole city of Arlington, Texas, the State of Texas and the United States come into their full redemptive purpose. He also has a zeal for developing a strong covenant relationship with the First Nations people. He desires to witness the releasing of the full destiny of God into their lives as the first peoples of our nation.

He is the author of <u>Return of the Priests</u>, a book declaring that God is restoring a kingdom of priests in our generation-not a priesthood defined by clerical collars and religious rituals. Rather it is a priesthood of everyday people walking intimately with God, who act and speak with life-changing authority in their homes, neighborhoods, and workplaces.

He is also the author of <u>Keeper of the Keys</u>, a book that shares how God is opening doors so that His kingdom can come forth into this earth. But He needs gatekeepers -those who will open the doors of His power, presence and transforming life to come into family, workplace, city, state and nation. You will discover in these pages that you are a Keeper of the Keys. He has empowered you to be a gatekeeper. Like Nehemiah and Peter, you have been given keys that will unlock the glory of the Lord in your region. It is also available on Amazon.

He is married to Kay Sanders Schlueter, and they have three grown children: Josh, Katie and her husband Tim, and Amy and her husband Allan. The couple has five grandchildren.

Contact:
Thomas Schlueter Prince of Peace
House of Prayer
Texas Apostolic Prayer Network
1712 Herschel Street
Arlington, Texas 76010
pt4texas@gmail.com
www.texasapn.com

OTHER BOOKS BY THE AUTHOR

Both are available at Amazon in Paperback and Kindle

www.ingramcontent.com/pod-product-compliance
Lightning Source LLC
Chambersburg PA
CBHW060218170726
48004CB00014B/540